Praise for Staying Put

"Duo Dickinson is not only a talented architect and author, but also an irrepressible spirit who isn't afraid to tweak the whiskers of the king or call a spade a spade. This book is not only about a subject that is extremely timely, given the state of both the housing market and the economy, but also an absolute delight to read.

How many books do you know that can give you multiple and frequent full-throttle belly laughs while delivering basic and simple advice about how to make friends with, and even come to love, the house that until recently you'd imagined you'd be moving up from sometime in the not-too-distant future? Duo's latest opus does just that. I loved every page of this fact-filled, practical book. It's worth your time to read, even if you're not planning to remodel any time soon. But my guess is that by the time you're finished, you may be closer to a remodeling than you thought."

> **—Sarah Susanka, FAIA**—architect and author of *Not So Big Remodeling* and *The Not So Big House* series

"Could there be a more perfect book for this American moment? Figuring out how to hunker down happily—replacing unsustainable fantasies of shelter porn with long-term, real-life shelter love—is the new name of the game, and I know of no more expert, charming guide than Duo Dickinson."

> **—Kurt Andersen,** host of public radio's *Studio 360* and author of *Heyday*

"People used to fix up their houses mainly to impress potential buyers—whose standards, they figured, were higher. But nowadays nobody's buying, so why not impress yourself? If you follow Duo Dickinson's excellent advice, you'll end up with a house you won't want to leave even to go to the grocery store."

> **—David Owen,** staff writer for *The New Yorker* and author of *Green Metropolis: Why Living Smaller, Living Closer, and Driving Less are the Keys to Sustainability*

staying put

Remodel Your House to Get the Home You Want

DUO DICKINSON

The Taunton Press

To my clients: They have blessed my life and work, and made this book possible.

The Taunton Press
Inspiration for hands-on living®

Taunton Press, Inc., 63 South Main Street,
PO Box 5506, Newtown, CT 06470-5506
e-mail: tp@taunton.com

Editor: Peter Chapman
Copy editor: Candace B. Levy
Cover and interior design: Laura Palese
Layout: Laura Palese

The following names/manufacturers appearing in *Staying Put* are trademarks:
iPad®, La Choy®, Realtor®

Library of Congress Cataloging-in-Publication Data

Dickinson, Duo.
  Staying put : remodel your house to get the home you want / author, Duo Dickinson.
    p. cm.
  ISBN 978-1-60085-364-7
  1. Dwellings--Remodeling. 2. Interior decoration. I. Title. II. Title: Remodel your house to get the home you want.
  TH4816.D54 2011
  690'.80288--dc23
                      2011030919

Printed in the United States of America
10 9 8 7 6 5 4 3 2 1

Acknowledgments

The Taunton Press had the courage and insight to support a new kind of home design book—one that has energy, substance, and innovation in its concept, design, and product—all during a difficult time for publishers. Maria Taylor was instrumental in taking a leap of faith, and I am deeply grateful. Peter Chapman is simply the best editor I have ever met, and it is only due to him that this text avoids pretentious affect—well, mostly . . .

Three women were essential in the hard writing slog: Cheryl Alison, Shannon Romanos, and Amanda Baker, and I thank them for keeping pace with the flow of words and ideas. Most important to everything beyond text was Ariel Torres, who shepherded every jot and tittle of artwork you see before you.

I have known Mick Hales for 28 years; he is a dear friend whose photographs are a gift to our culture and to this book.

As always, my office has borne the brunt of my distraction with all non-design activities, and I specifically thank Brian Ross, Nicole Girard, and Sean Rowe, who bore the brunt of that brunt.

My family is used to my polyglot overscheduling, and this book took time from my wife, Liz, and sons, Will and Sam, that cannot be justified, only tolerated.

My greatest gratitude goes to those who make my professional life a humbling gift of trust and friendship—the hundreds of families who entrust their domestic dreams to my embrace. That faith goes beyond the unavoidable financial and functional risks of an outsider getting quite personal with their largest possession. Their abiding trust is the essence of my life's work: building love into the safe harbor of home.

about this book

First, you should know that, for good or ill, every project in this book had me as its architect (a built-in or two were designed by others).

The budgets of the projects presented are intentionally varied: some are tiny, some are quite large, with costs ranging from under $100 to over $1,000 per square foot of remodeled space. The locations range from isolated exurban homes to in-city apartments and everything in between.

Any book has a finite number of pages. In trying to contain all the written and graphic material within the book's covers, it quickly became clear that some worthy content would not make it into print form. Fortunately, this book lends itself perfectly to multiple platforms of availability, and the material that would not fit (and much more) can be found at www.stayingput.com.

On the website you will find more photos, more projects, more rules ("Duo's Do's and Don'ts"), and more musings on prototypic house styles ("Find Your House") and elements that have disappeared from homes that people want today ("Where Are They Now?"). Look for the weblinks throughout the book.

▶ go to www. staying put.com

Contents

Housebound in America

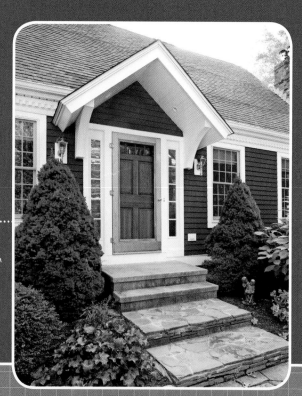

A new entry can make a quiet Cape "yours."

There are over 80 million single-family homes in America, and it's estimated that 18 million of these are "under water," meaning the mortgage is larger than the value of the house. Millions of families feel trapped, living a life sentence of domestic frustration in homes that do not work for them while being unable to move to solve the problems they confront on a daily basis.

This book offers tangible hope for getting the home you want from the house you have.

Families now have to focus on the homes they have rather than assume a lifelong leapfrog up a never-ending path of escalating home values. The newly imposed long-term commitment to our homes is closer to the historic norm than the distorted housing markets of recent years. Families are rediscovering the traditional tether to home sweet home as a specific fixed place rather than a movable stage set for our belongings.

Staying put is far closer to the American tradition of the family home as part of what a family really is.

Since World War II, people have never stopped spending on their homes. I have been an architect for 30 years thriving through three economic cycles, from boom to bust and all the transitions in between. For every other housing bust, one or two sections of the United States escaped the general downturn: Oil money saved much of the South in the early 1980s, the tech boom saved much of the West in the late 1980s. But the present depressed state in housing value is truly national, just as the last decade's housing bubble was a national juggernaut of overvaluation and irrational exuberance. Because of its massive scale, this period of reduced expectations and great consumer fear is a longer, deeper, and more depressing malaise than any of the other building busts since World War II.

Having designed about 600 homes over these three decades (new, remodeled, or completely renovated), I know that housing consumers can be deeply depressed but they are never hopeless. Our houses are just too important to us—personally, culturally, and economically—to have a general economic condition pull the rug out from acting on our fondest hopes.

There are silver linings in dark economic times—competitive costs, available contractors, and, most important, a rational sense of a home's real value and a clear sense of what the costs are to get houses to work for those who live in them. When money was inexpensive to borrow and the home you had in hand was always rising in value, the worth of your home (and what you thought about spending to improve it) was not much of a limitation on your expectations. It was guilt-free binge-building gluttony on a massive scale, but now we all must go on a morning-after diet regimen.

It's time to see the value in the can-do spirit that spiraled out of control for a while. There is little in the material world that we hold as dear as the place we rest our heads and welcome our families and friends. Our homes are undeniably essential to our quality of life, especially when times get dicey. This book will empower you to see where you can change your home to embrace how you live without going broke.

Staying put

One of our most basic human instincts is to nest—it is literally a genetic prime directive, a value system that has not been celebrated in recent American history. Traditionally, we have adapted, renewed, and revitalized our existing homes, rather than search for the "salvation" of the next new home.

before & AFTER

Many older homes are bought more for their neighborhoods and locations rather than for the houses themselves. Typically built closer to urban centers, the homes are on nicer pieces of land and have the quality of landscape that only decades of growth can provide. Here, a 19th-century Colonial subtly accepts a new mud-room entry (at left).

Before the explosion of suburbia and waves of bedroom communities pushed people away from our cities, the vast majority of people who owned single-family homes had them not as a status symbol to be traded in for a better model or as an investment strategy. Until the 1950s owning a home meant creating "the family home," a permanent part of the family tree. It was a backbone to the arc of a family's history and identity. Where we lived had a similar level of permanence as the genetic makeup that kept the family's characteristics distinct and formed the family identity. Before World War II, families invested equity into their homes to make them larger or more impressive or occasionally to move the home to a better place rather than the pump, dump, and run strategy of late-20th-century suburbia.

People came to expect that they could manifest their best hopes and dreams in where they live—a unique concept before World War II for the majority of people who rented rather than owned their dwelling. Even in the worst economic times, homes served as a good place to put your hard-earned money over a period of decades. No matter how much the value of your home fluctuated, if you bought it correctly and you didn't owe too much on it, it rarely sank below the amount of money that you had invested in it. Until now.

The most recent downturn broke the upward line of house values for the foreseeable future. Homes will probably begin their upward march again because something as inherently valuable to human beings cannot be denied. As the population increases, we need more places for families to live and if families can own homes rather than rent, they will. Even at the lowest end of our most recent economic condition, over 300,000 houses were built in any given year.

There are close to 115 million households in America, and about 80 million freestanding houses are no longer seen as fungible as a block of stock to be bought and sold on a commodity basis. Consequently, we have returned to a mind-set that we haven't seen since the GIs came back after VJ Day. It is a mind-set so basic that it's hard to understand how we got away from it: a home is part of who a family is, that the love and attention we visit upon family members can have a collateral reality in the home that they are committed to.

The disconnect that developed whereby homes were simply another investment (albeit our most important one) almost killed the homesteading tradition in recent American culture. As the 20th century progressed, almost no one lived in their homes their entire lives. More people felt empowered by the serial monogamy of moving from

▶ go to www.stayingput.com for more before and after photos

one place to another to piggyback onto the value that had been created in the last home to reach for an even greater net value of the next home.

That focus outward meant that homes were inherently devalued in terms of their emotional presence in our lives. Very few of us married our high school sweetheart. Similarly, house shopping felt more like speed dating than an old-time, long-term engagement in which our commitment was in stages, and ultimately a wedding meant a permanent relationship. We learned that we could actually divorce ourselves from our homes, move on, and start another very important but almost certainly limited relationship.

As many of us found out in our marriages, the lack of permanence in the horizon of our commitment made many of our decisions shaky, hollow, and inevitably sad. Permanence has two faces. It can make you feel powerless and a victim of fate, or it can ground you and give you the confidence that where you are is where you want to be and that the decisions you make have a permanent platform

A simple Cape was extended to allow changes in use (a master bedroom down, at right) and protection from the elements (a new roof over the front door, center).

The best renovations are not the ones that enable a home to be sold to strangers for the highest price in the shortest time. The best renovations are the ones that make you and your family feel like you've created a *home* out of a box. The best renovations join houses to their sites. The best renovations make living easier and happier.

for your personal expression. Our homes have transitioned back to a place where permanence rather than superficial empowerment inspires personal expression.

In many ways it is back to the future for the American homeowner. The "new" economic paradigm of the previous 50 years was based on a mass buy-in to an unending move-up mentality. The home was not only the fundamental engine of personal economic fortune hunting but also of national house building companies, whose equity is traded on the open market, pushing homes away from our hearts and into our wallets.

This book can show you that despite the obvious physical misfit of living in homes designed 70 years ago, you can change your home to fit you. The sense of commitment that 19th century homeowners felt can actually create a refreshing level of resourcefulness and inspiration. Overcoming a misfit may not have the same sense of instant

Staying put does not
mean standing pat.

gratification as trading in your car, but changing things for the better permanently, knowing that you'll bask in that change for decades and not just a couple of years, not only raises the ante of commitment but also of reward.

We have been in a dating relationship with our homes. We now have a shotgun marriage of necessity that may just prove to be the love relationship of a lifetime. It is time to commit to where we live rather than have our way with our homes and depart. It's time to give our family a home rather than a stage for an episode in a series of venues. It is time to learn what families for centuries already knew, that our homes are as fundamental to our lives as our family tree. Staying put does not mean standing pat.

What's needed?

Even with the best of intentions, residential remodels can create misfits that ruin the character of your home and create more problems than they solve. Think about the cute Cape rendered into an awkward afterthought by the massive box add-on great room. Without the perspective of thoughtful design, a remodeled home can actually be more expensive to heat, cool, and maintain than the original home, and with a larger indebtedness and mortgage payment to boot.

How do you avoid these pitfalls and still make a home that is ill-fitting (and often beginning to fall apart) accommodate the needs of your family in an economy that

ABOVE LEFT: Sometimes space needs to be extended to capture views to the outside world.

ABOVE RIGHT: Raising the roof over an existing space (here, an existing garage was given over to a kitchen and dining area) can make a tight home feel and function bigger.

doesn't allow you to buy, sell, or trade your way up and out? Knowledge creates hope. This is a book of options and solutions for people who are desperate to transform the buildings they are resigned to live in into homes that fit the way they live and reflect their values.

What are we up against?

Classic off-the-rack home designs were formulated in eras when family patterns were very different from today's. They bind in the bath and closet, they are loose in the formal dining room, and they are MIA when it comes to a mudroom or eat-in kitchen. They leak treated air, warmed or chilled, like the Nixon White House leaked scandals. And, yes, they are often tacky, if not downright ugly, and have often been "renovated" to make them far, far worse than their original misfit designs.

Our Capes closet us, our Colonials force us to walk through walls, our Ranches create a slip-sliding tightness of rooms that frustrates the way most of us live. Ozzie and Harriet did not have to adjust to modern realities. Children are overprogrammed with unending activities that leave heaps of detritus in their wake. We recycle and want to use less energy. We contend with more than one career and bring our parents and/or grown-up children back within our walls; many of us now require a home office or two. And since we all stopped smoking and started working out, we should outlive Ozzie and Harriet, giving our joints time to betray the rest of our bodies, so our houses also need to adapt to our extended life spans.

where are they now?

We learn more from our mistakes than when we do just enough to avoid disaster and muddle through. But to move beyond muddling through and to change what we know is just not working, we need to play Monday morning quarterback.

Sometimes you have to go too far to learn what makes sense. In every building boom since World War II, people have built too much too fast. The first decade of the 21st century was no exception. Many people who overspent in ways that made no sense are now having their noses rubbed into the folly of their misjudgment. But the upside of other people's mistakes is that you can benefit from them.

Nothing teaches as well as a bad example, and over the last decade there were bad examples aplenty to learn from, including showroom kitchens, great rooms, and palatial master suites. These essential elements of our homes were all miscalculated in ways that should provide a reality check for anyone thinking about renovating today. (Look for "Where Are They Now?" sidebars throughout the book and at www.stayingput.com.)

Now what?

Until recently, homeowners assumed their *next* house could fix the problems of their *present* house and that solution was just a simple transaction or two away. No more. The intellectually lazy, environmentally suspect, and economically unsustainable mass delusion of an ever-expanding American housing market is justifiably dead. In its place comes a more nimble, nuanced, and resourceful nation of homeowners.

Our cultural hubris has had a dramatic economic buzz kill, but the lessons learned point the way to a reality-based, value-centered building ethic. Given the overbuilding and underthinking of the last decade, our moral, fiscal, and practical compasses point to an era of starting with what we have in hand. Renovation of the home you cannot leave may not be the ultimate experience of ego projection, but the empowerment of taking control is undeniable if you have crafted a thoughtfully applied strategy based on knowledge and creativity.

Working with existing buildings requires more patience, knowledge, and craftiness than the tear-down mentality of unfettered expansion or building on a naked site. But the advantages of sober thinking and value-conscious building are obvious and will be revealed, explained, and expounded in this book.

20th-century homes based on 18th-century prototype house designs don't cut it functionally in the 21st century.

1

Get your act together

Sitting in a flood plain tight to zoning setbacks, this remodel had to be vetted on many levels beyond passing muster visually and functionally.

Most of us glide through the relationship with our home simply hoping for the best.

A home is the ultimate financial and functional can of worms that you may not want to open up for fear it will break the bank and make your life a misery. For people who want to continue to live in denial, homes are a little like the extremely odd relative who moves in with you: quiet most of the time but every once in a while there's a grand-mal meltdown that you can't avoid and have to deal with—a pipe bursts, your roof develops a leak, or you can't open the window in your bedroom. If you want to continue to kick the can down the road, you will be sentenced to living in fear and throwing money away on stop-gap repairs in crisis-management mode versus fixing the cause of your home's problems.

A Bungalow that was mangled in the 1950s is now integrated, newly detailed, and focused on a single front door rather than the split entries of its previous cut-up occupancy.

It used to be that if a home turned out to be too much of a problem, you could simply sell it and move on to the next one. But that scenario typically doesn't work anymore. So for people who previously never considered it an option, one has been imposed on them—take charge. Fix the house so it doesn't get in the way of your life and, just maybe, make the place where you live a place you love.

It's a big step, not unlike deciding to have children or changing your career, as renovating your home to make it yours becomes a job unto itself. Just like pregnancy, there is a finish line. All projects do come to an end one way or

Take charge: Fix the house so it doesn't get in the way of your life.

another so that throughout all the anxiety, effort, pain, and frustration, there is light at the end of the tunnel. And at the end of the tunnel, if you've hired the right people and kept your head clear, you'll have a house that not only has fewer ongoing, nagging issues but also could be a fun place to come home to. In this chapter, we'll look at some of the areas where you can take control of your domestic destiny and some of the ways in which you can make the ride less bumpy and more productive.

Get your mind-set set

Once you've decided you're in for the ride of renovation, it's time to get the guardrails of grounded perspective in place.

1. Cost is king. As soon as possible, you need to get to the point where you know the investment makes sense. Remember that nothing you do short of painting your home or perhaps adding an inexpensive deck will actually recoup the dollar investment if you sell right after you've finished. However, when you execute a project that increases your home's value less than 50 percent of your investment, you should simply make sure that you want the feature so much that you're willing to take a financial bath if you ever go to resell it. Architects and builders can blue-sky costs and real estate brokers and appraisers can blue-sky the net impact on your home's worth once you can clearly define what needs doing.

2. Get real. Think about how you actually live versus the way you think you *should* live. Renovating a home will never make you pick up your dirty clothes or make you a good cook or a better parent. A renovation should take how you live now and make it flow without frustration, be more organized, and—we hope—a delight to behold.

3. Time is your friend. The more time you spend planning and evaluating your design, the cheaper your project will be. When you take the time to plan, think, and work with those who are knowledgeable in design and products, you should be able to estimate the cost of your options. The more time you spend looking at options, the better the bang for the buck.

The more time you spend planning and evaluating your design, the cheaper your project will be.

4. Knowledge is happiness. Whether it's getting a better sense of what an architect or builder is talking about, understanding the appropriate cost expectations, or just comprehending the world of construction, any time you invest in obtaining the deep background info will make you less fearful and more positive in your outlook. The lingo and processes of designing, getting permits, and building can be learned before you go through the actual act of remodeling.

5. The unaffordable perfect should never prevent the affordable good. You seldom get everything you want (either in scope or in quality) when you renovate. In other words, money will always end up affecting your fondest dreams.

Remember that renovation is a lot like a second (or fourth) marriage: You are already grounded in the reality of the situation you're in, and you should have a tempered, reality-based expectation that you will find happiness but not the unrealistic expectation that you will be living in a perfected state.

Look before you leap

No matter how great your drawings are, no matter how many renderings or models a designer or architect makes, the risks are always there that all the time, money, and effort you spend on your remodel are going to create something that will not turn out the way you want it to. But you can narrow that window of potential disappointment.

As computer programmers are fond of saying, "Garbage in, garbage out." The only way for you to take out the trash of fear is to gain confidence that you know the objective essentials of home remodeling. That's probably why you have this book in your hands, pay attention to shelter magazines, and watch TV programs that deal with houses. If you don't already have a knowledge base, now is the time to get one.

DUO'S DO'S & DON'TS

Your house is a mirror, not a 12-step program

Whoever you are is what your house should be. If you don't like yourself, your house will not make you like yourself any better. If your family is dysfunctional, a new home will not pull it together. So any renovation you attempt as a psychological balm is destined to fail. Know that what makes your family and friends love you is you, not who you want to be, not what you could have been, and definitely not what your home should be. The best remodels are the ones that take whoever you are and celebrate it. Renovations will not succeed in forcing some sense of order on a life that is inherently disordered or clarity to a life that is mercurially confused.

▶ go to **www. staying put.com** for more of Duo's Do's and Don'ts

In a free-market society where the consumer is king, we're used to being offered options with hard price tags. Whether buying a car, a couch, or a TV, we can choose from a menu of à la carte upgrades that are clearly defined and priced and whose implications are self-evident. In home remodeling, the opposite is true. Every possible aspect of a renovation is a question, not an answer. Although a knowable price range is possible, there is no guarantee what any renovation will cost until the project is defined, drawn, and reviewed by builders who have skin in the game and need to be accurate in that cost analysis. If they underprice, they will lose their business; if they play it safe and pad the cost, they won't get work if the job is competitively bid. Despite all efforts to provide accurate descriptions of what needs doing and how much it should cost, in reality, the final budget of any construction project is determined only once you start building and find out the hidden costs.

The final budget of any construction project is determined only once you start building and find out the hidden costs.

With knowledge comes power. And the most important knowledge you have is the specific understanding of the possibilities and problems that your own house now has. No matter what bright ideas a builder, architect, or designer might have, if, for you, an element of your home

Adding a new stair to this simple Victorian home opened up the interior. The addition was made possible by extending the new front-door space under the existing porch roof.

ain't broke, don't fix it. On the other hand, if something makes you crazy, but does not bother the vanilla house shopper or sell-anything real estate agent, fix it anyway.

No home is perfect for its occupants unless they've designed it from scratch, and even then it probably still needs some fine-tuning. A stock plan designed for people living 50 years or 100 years ago can't meet the expectations of families living in a time when the characteristics of the American family have changed dramatically. Homes that were designed when oil was 20¢ a gallon don't address the long-term economic reality that energy is not going to get any cheaper in the near term. Closets sized to handle one season's worth of clothing or kitchens that are shut off from the rest of the house are simply out of touch with how people use houses today.

find your home: the cape

The Cape is probably as close to an uber house as one can get: a simple rectangle with a gable roof; a centered entry and windows; a chimney at either end or, more commonly, in the center; and, in later models, shed, doghouse, or larger gable dormers sprouting from the roof.

If you're thinking of remodeling a Cape, try to use its undeniably iconic shape as a springboard for some functional liberation and aesthetic zest. The back side of a Cape, almost completely unseen from the street, can go a little bit crazy. A single large dormer or rear-projecting wing can make the house into an architectural changeling—controlled, symmetrical, and squinty-eyed to the street, with the rollicking, guffawing celebratory backside facing the harbor of informal suburban life.

Unless you are a historicist freak (or possess a true antique) there is literally nothing sacred about most Capes. In fact, many Capes have been turned into a wide variety of other homes over the centuries, including Saltboxes (doubling up the top), Garrison Colonials (going up and out to the sides), and long attenuated "Big House, Back House, Little House, Barn" rambling farmhouse structures. In short, don't feel beholden to the Cape unless you are simply in love with its form.

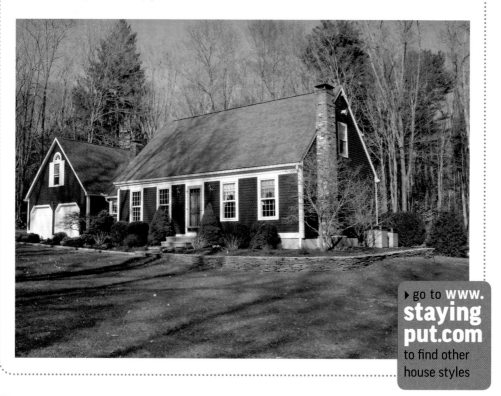

▶ go to www.
**staying
put.com**
to find other
house styles

Money pit or silk purse?

Is your home worth renovating? In this section, we'll look at the typical areas where homes and their sites can become your worst enemy. Some may be terminally devastating to your hopes of detoxing your environment. Other symptoms are as benign as dandruff—an annoyance, but manageable at a reasonable cost.

ABOVE: A steep change of level and some extreme plant overgrowth made getting to this home's front door unnecessarily awkward. (To see the fix, turn to p. 243.)

Your lot

Your site determines so much about your home, and its seemingly unchangeable characteristics demand that you pay attention to it. One of the key characteristics is access, and the greatest complication to access is grade—that is, the hilly parts. Your site may be so problematic that you should think twice about investing a lot of money in a remodel that's just too hard to get to. If your home is on the down low or is too high and mighty, your site may require huge amounts of regrading, blasting, and so on, just to make a bad driveway better.

The goal is safety. New homes built under present codes limit the slope of any driveway to 15 degrees (which is relatively shallow). In addition, you really should get to level *before* you get to the street and *before* you get to your house. A driveway that doesn't allow you to turn around and drive front ways to the street (versus backing out) is a tough thing to accept for you but worse for a visitor. Conceptually, fixing a driveway that's too steep can be simple (bringing in fill) or very complicated (rerouting and

before & **AFTER**

An addition to this classic Ranch set on a hillside connects the living floor directly to the landscape (right), while new siding and windows create a depth of detail the existing house lacked.

evaluate your house

One of the biggest advantages of remodeling in place is that if you've lived in your home for any length of time, you know exactly what your home's problems and potentials are. No amount of on-paper analysis can replace the direct, real-time, full-scale, year-round knowledge born of experience. Here are some mind-sets for your evaluation:

blasting). You likely won't be able to evaluate the potential for problems unless you consult with a surveyor or an architect for some hard-number, on-paper analysis.

SEPTIC Where your water and waste goes can sometimes tell you if your home is worth renovating. If you have a septic system (versus a hook-up to town sewers) and you want to add a bedroom or two or add on near that septic system, you need to review how it limits you. Two things have worked in opposite directions in the world of waste in the last 20 years. On the one hand, new technologies have made septic systems exquisitely small and this helps (but those systems are pricey—upward of $30,000). On the other hand, septic codes have gotten far more restrictive. Depending on who is doing the regulating, many controlling agencies

DUO'S DO'S & DON'TS

You can't fight the site and stay cheap

The vast majority of American homes are sited on their lots without any thought to the views. This is because most American homes are built from stock plans that assume a flat site that has a street in front of it and a yard behind it. When you ram a simple rectangular box into a hill that flies off to one side, all kinds of weirdness can happen: Decks launch out into space, windows face hillsides, great views are unseen, and rainwater flows where it shouldn't. There are ways to make your house better connect with the existing site's topography, trees, views, and so on, but it takes a lot more effort than simply removing a wall or adding a bay window.

- Does natural light fall into your house the way you want it to? Is there too much of it? Is there too little?

- How do you enter your house? Directly from the car? From the sidewalk?

- Where do you want the bedrooms in your home? Separate or integrated? Next to your children's rooms or away from them?

- Does your bathroom allow you to do what you need to do when you need to do it, or does it frustrate or embarrass you?

- What role does the TV have in your life? Central or secondary?

- What role does the computer have in your life? Central or secondary?

- Is energy efficiency an imperative or simply a nice thing to consider?

- Are there areas of your home that need continual maintenance?

- Is your stairway somewhat terrifying to use?

- When you want to go outside, do you have to walk a great distance or is there a quick connection?

- Are there doors that always stick? Windows that have ceased to operate?

require the use of your existing virgin subsoil (you can't bring in any new dirt). In addition, most municipalities require that you design not only for the capacity you need now but also for a future separate system designed with your specific subsoils in mind for when your system fails many years from now.

Septic repairs are sometimes allowed for renovations, but don't count on it. Adding just one bedroom (yes, they don't judge you on the number of bathrooms you have but on the number of bedrooms) can mean your entire existing septic system may need to meet today's codes. Here's where you can get clever: *Meet code* doesn't necessarily mean installing an entire new septic system for your home if the existing one works. You can advocate for a separate, additional, smaller system for your new bedroom and see if the local sanitarian agrees. Further, there are many ways to count bedrooms. If your children can handle sharing, there is no reason you can't simply remove a wall between two small bedrooms and make one large double sleeping space and then add a guest bedroom somewhere else and your existing septic system may be able to remain as is.

Be aware that you must keep your septic system a required distance from your home and other parts of your site. First, keeping it away from your house is keyed to your basement type and whether you have a perimeter drain; similarly, the system needs to be held away from your property lines. If you have ledge, wetlands, or steep slopes on your site, they can all limit where your septic work can happen. A surveyor can help you see what's possible and what's not. If you are thinking about using geothermal energy for your house, realize those wells or fields also need to respect your septic.

UTILITIES A good home inspector, builder, or architect can immediately let you know the status of your utilities (the electrical, plumbing, and heating systems). Most homes built before World War II that haven't been upgraded are usually compromised in several ways. The electrical capacity might be under 100 amps (inadequate for the huge array of electronic appliances in most people's homes today and simply a nonstarter if you want air-conditioning). In addition, in vintage homes, the power comes into a box that has fuses rather than circuit breakers in it. The electricity that comes out of that fuse box is broken into a minimum number of circuits, often without separate circuits for individual appliances (now a code requirement) let alone separate "home run" circuits dedicated to electronics that are sensitive to power surges (like high-tech TVs, computers, and so on). And there are still houses with combustible insulation and ungrounded service, which are quick tickets to tragedy.

BELOW: Replacing a wall with a dropped beam (upper left) and a closed exterior wall with windows simultaneously opens up this kitchen to the house and to the landscape.

Every electrical design on paper gets tossed out once the framing is done

Architects and interior designers are quite clever and can see around corners and visualize the way things will look. But no one can visualize exactly what a home's interior is like, despite all computer program promotions to the contrary. There's nothing like walking into the full-size, reality-based interior of your home and seeing how the natural light comes in and what the walls shield and reveal to completely change any lighting scenario that might have been drawn. Therefore, even if you have a full budget number for fixed lighting and outlets, no matter how great the architect or designer or electrician on the case, you should assert your authority to demand changes you can see only once your project's framing is up and before the electrician installs anything. There's no cost to changing locations if nothing's been located, but once things are in, there will be an unending debate as to how much the changes will cost—a debate you will lose.

Water lines that come into many homes built before World War II can be ¾ in. in diameter or less versus the 1 in. or even 1½ in. that many homes require now to have adequate water flow. If you have a well for water, it affects where you can put a new or updated septic system; if you want a new well, it needs to be located where your septic isn't by a goodly amount.

Existing oil tanks become a real issue when you want to renovate because they are sometimes generations old, may be buried, leak like a sieve, and generate enormous remediation costs not covered by most insurance policies.

TREES A house nestled under a tree is the very definition of picturesque. Unfortunately, when tree limbs go over roofs, those roofs are damaged by the unending dampness and by the composting of the on-roof organic material that spews during the tree's reproductive process. All that dampness and organic material ends up creating mold, mildew, and rot for wood roofs; the presence of all this schmutz also accelerates the degradation of asphalt roofs and ultimately can cause the deterioration of skylights, dormers, and the flashing around your chimney. The frailty of the tree's age when combined with wind or snow often allows very large limbs to fall, causing damage uncovered by any insurance policy. Trees can grow to destroy your septic field

Trees provide welcome shade in summer, but they may also be destroying the roof over your house.

too. Trees can stabilize hilly sites, but they can completely destabilize your driveway. The good news is that trimming and outright removal are options if you need to de-tree to remodel, but verify if your town regulates tree removal.

save that tree

If you want to preserve a tree during construction, you should allow zero activity around it any closer to the area covered by the limbs of the tree (a.k.a. the drip line); this is not only for what you build but also during construction. Maples and other trees that have shallow roots are easily damaged and are often killed by just driving construction equipment across the roots.

Relocating even a medium-size tree is excruciatingly expensive. Thus if a tree is going to end up being in close proximity to what you are doing, it might make sense to limb away subordinate branches and feed the tree with fertilizers belowgrade the season before you initiate construction. Trees can be saved in most instances, but there are times when your renovation will have the effect of an herbicide. It is a balancing act, and you have to decide which is more important to you: the needs of your house or the fact that you would be killing something that may have been around longer than you have.

ABOVE & RIGHT: The best view in the house may be from the attic; and, as an added advantage, creating a finished space out of raw structure is often cheaper than building new.

VIEWS If you have a view, it is probably one of your home's greatest assets, and remodeling should take full advantage of that asset. It's pretty easy to gain access to views simply by chopping bigger holes in your house. Your home's interior should be rethought to take full advantage of any compelling views you might have. Houses built from stock plans tend to put any number of small view blockers in front of those vistas (bathrooms, closets, and bedrooms).

Your foundation/basement

The way your house is supported by the site is a critical factor in evaluating its suitability for remodeling. Water getting into your basement may not be as troubling as a leaky roof, but it can still give you doubts about renovating. There are several ways to keep water out of your basement. Most experts recommend installing gutters if your home does not have them. While that may help in certain conditions, as with an older foundation (fieldstone or block) that has no curtain drain or damp-proofing, gutters don't always work and tend to overflow in high-volume rains or get ripped off by snow and ice. If your house is in a depressed area of your site, it gets harder to keep groundwater away, even with effective guttering.

A better option is to regrade around your house to keep the rain water that does come off your roof or the surface water flowing around your home from coming close to it. Once water is directed away from your house it has to go somewhere—to a catch basin to disperse below grade away from your location or just downhill from your house if the grading allows.

If you have a chronic leaky basement due not only to ground-water or runoff but also to a high water table (and you have unlimited

BELOW: Wide eaves do a better job of keeping water out of the basement than do gutters.

Gutters are of the devil

Gutters and leaders are devoutly to be avoided. They make construction more expensive now and in the out years. Gutters do control most of the water that runs off your roof, but not all of it. Most gutters are set 1 in. or 2 in. higher than the leading edge of the roofline and form a perfect scoop that holds all ice and snow in place, ultimately forcing water to back up underneath your roof shingles and into your house. More propitious for installers, the weight of snow and ice terminally bends or rips off gutters on a regular basis. If gutters are installed correctly (lower than the roof edge), heavy rain water will sheet off the edge of the gutter and erode the ground plane around your facade. They do control water that might otherwise get in your basement, but that is a last-ditch effort when regrading has failed.

You should never walk into a house without a gable over your head because snow doesn't respect gutters. You should grade and plant around your house to prevent erosion from the start, gutters or not. And you should have some sort of foundation water-control systems (watertight coatings, a subsurface curtain drain, or a perimeter drain to get water away from your basement), gutters or not. If your eaves are of an adequate size, the splashback of water on a facade can be controlled. Assuming that gutters will work for all of these things is a little bit like asking the plastic poncho that you buy for $2 at a ballgame to be your raincoat for the next 20 years.

It pays to take advantage of the landscape. Here, an existing basement was opened up to the lower driveway by way of retaining walls and foundation reinforcement. A new two-car garage was created without changing the historic home's facade.

funds), you could pull dirt away from your foundation walls and waterproofing and install a perimeter drain below the level of that basement floor. Facing a choice between a $15,000- to $50,000-drainage-remediation project and a new kitchen, it's pretty clear which way most homeowners would go.

In this scenario (water rising up from below, versus soaking in from above), such a system can actually draw water to your basement so, alternatively, sump pumps might be the only solution—and they are significantly cheaper than a full-perimeter drainage/waterproofing retrofit. It is probably a good idea to put in two or three sump pumps in your house for redundancy if one breaks down and to provide an integrated connection to a generator for when the power goes out. This all involves money but far less than if a finished basement gets flooded out and needs a repair that is not covered by insurance.

Any perforation of your foundation wall for pipes (water, oil, gas, sleeves for electrical wires) may also leak, but a thorough raking and recaulking of any gap that is around these perforations is a quick and easy fix. What is not an easy fix, however, are fieldstone, brick, or old concrete block foundation walls where the connecting mortar has failed. Every seam is a potential leak so each joint has to be perfect for your basement not to leak. It is only partially effective to regrout on the inside. If the foundation is in terrible condition, you probably have to bite the bullet and hit the problem from the outside. And this level of cost might just be a deal-breaker.

SETTLEMENT If you see cracks in your home's walls, it's natural to fear that your foundation is failing, but settlement occurs only when your house's foundation has failed to a resting point of stability. Settlement is more common in older homes where not much thought was put into foundations—especially in antique homes that have huge central chimneys that not only supported their own mass but also the weight of the house (now a code no-no).

The vast majority of cracks that you see in a recently built home's above-basement walls are due to shrinkage of the home's framing, not foundation movement. For the last 40 years or so, the trees that are harvested for framing

Facing a choice between a $15,000- to $50,000-drainage-remediation project and a new kitchen, it's pretty clear which way most homeowners would go.

find your home: the colonial

The Colonial is the mac and cheese of our culture's domestic architecture fare, the essential baseline for almost all residential thinking. When the early colonists came to North America, they had to put a roof over their heads quickly to survive. They had to come up with a dwelling that shed water and would protect them against animals, weather, and anyone who wanted to steal what they had taken so much courage and effort to build.

Given those circumstances, the original Colonial homes had to be built quickly. As a result, the houses were rectangular and symmetrical and had a gable roof and central line of support for the floors that paralleled those rectangular walls. The openings in a Colonial are literally by rote, with evenly spaced small windows and the front door dead center on the street-facing facade.

The Colonial Revival suburban aesthetic has many variations, including Federal, Saltbox, and Garrison, but the Center Hall has been the easiest to market universally. It has a double-height, longer face to the street and narrower gabled ends facing the side yards. The rectangular box opens into a narrow middle bay that has a straight-run staircase to one side and a hallway to the other, with walls on either side carrying the weight of the floors above. Like so many types of American domestic architecture, this small acorn has exploded into gigantism and Center Hall Colonials have been overbuilt.

The siding of a Colonial is either painted or clear-finished wood or its artificial simulation (clapboard or shingles), often with shutters and paneled front doors, which are now often made with imitation products. Windows are always made with divided-lite panes (grilles in current parlance) and should be double-hung.

lumber have been grown with a version of arboreal steroids, then cut in adolescence, dried to a minimum standard, and used immediately. As a result, the wood used now is weaker and less stable than ever before. But other newer products used in framing have virtually zero moisture in them: beams made out of plywood-microlams and steel. The weak framing lumber described earlier is now often intertwined with these inert stronger products, so as time passes, the framing lumber parts move more than they used to and the engineered wood parts and steel beams hardly move at all. This movement is not settlement. It is your house's framing adapting to an average moisture level but also continuing to move as humidity varies in the atmosphere.

Even if your foundation has cracks, they are not necessarily related to the cracks you see in the rest of your house. Fine foundation wall and floor cracks can happen because concrete can crack as it cures. In well-crafted foundations, control joints are raked into walls and floors to isolate that cracking, but those grooves are not always found in mass-produced houses. Cracks could mean that during the process of putting

venting a basement

Dampness literally stinks. Mold, which is now considered to be life-threatening, begins with wetness. Basements with and without leaks are the primary harbor for dampness simply because air has moisture in it. The ground changes temperature very little so when the temperature starts rising above the level of deep dirt (50 degrees typically), your walls condense the air's moisture on their surface and that creates dampness.

If you smell mold, you need to address it before you dive into a full remodeling. There are two ways to fight it: either with dehumidifiers or by providing enough ventilation to dry out the condensation. Venting preempts a finished, heated, or air-conditioned basement, and you have to insulate your floor cavity—with a vapor barrier set up tight to the subfloor.

None of these moves is a budget-buster so getting rid of dampness is not a deal breaker. In any event, if you have an old house without a concrete slab (rock or dirt under foot), you also need to seal the dirt floor with both plastic and concrete. When your foundation is cut into ledge or tight subsoils, you may encounter radon, a toxic gas that should be vented mechanically with a timed fan and a vent pipe or two.

dirt back up against your house, there was some pressure added before the wall was stabilized by the home's framing. Bigger cracks (more than $\frac{1}{16}$ in. of separation) mean more movement and need professional assessment before you put money in your home. Cracks are never good but are often not a terrible problem if they aren't growing. If they continue to grow, bring in a structural engineer as soon as possible.

HEADROOM Lack of headroom in an older home's basement is a genetic flaw. If you're thinking of remodeling your basement, you have two choices to fix the problem. You can dig down to lower the floor and carefully add new support below your existing footings as you go (called "underpinning" by building nerds). Or you can lift your home up and add courses of concrete block around the perimeter of your foundation or stub your framing down to it. Either of these moves involve tens and tens of thousands of dollars.

Basements are extraordinarily good places to store things, especially if they are dry, but basements, after all, are just basements; places of limited view, access, and a fairly prison-like sense of hospitality. But on tight sites that offer little or no room for a shed or house expansion, getting your basement or crawlspace usable just might make sense.

Your floor plan

You and your family are the ones who determine whether a plan works or not. Things that frustrate one homeowner to distraction (a separate dining room, a cloistered living room, a kitchen that is completely open to either) may well be points of giddy delight for another.

before &
AFTER

There are a few things that no one likes, such as walking into a house and immediately seeing the powder room toilet or having to turn directions three times to get from the garage or the dining room into the kitchen. Beyond obvious practical difficulties, you are the one who should be determining the way you want the flow of your house to be, not an architect or a builder. Unless you want something extremely bizarre (a toilet sitting in the middle of a family room), you will have to live with your home now and into the foreseeable future, so resale

Taking out walls is almost always less expensive than adding on. This new kitchen was created in a tight living space and connected to an existing family room to create the type of open living scenario almost everyone prefers.

You are the one who should be determining the way you want the flow of your house to be, not an architect or a builder.

LEFT & ABOVE: Cabinetry conceals a washer and dryer that are set up at the most convenient level for access. The beadboard walls morph into doors to hide the insertion of appliances into a social space.

has ceased to be the prime motivator it once was. You are not crazy to want to get what you want if you can afford it. But there are some insights that most people overlook when they think about their homes. Sometimes the least exciting aspects of your home remodeling project can get you better results.

WHEN WALLS ARE A GOOD THING You've probably heard of the open classroom, a classic great idea promulgated in the 1970s that had a very short life. The gist was that walls destroyed children's creativity, overfocused them, caused boredom, and so on.

Truth be told, walls are often very good things. Schools put back almost all the walls that were taken out of them during the open classroom craze. The great room of the late 1970s and early 1980s was our home's open classroom, where virtually all family activity took place. Clearly, walls make sense when hyperfocused needs have to be accommodated (home office, homework area, and crafting area) or where there will be a perpetual and uncontrollable mess (preschool play area, home bill paying station, project table). The good news is that building walls that do not hold anything up (nonbearing partitions) is cheap—perhaps $50 a running foot for walls no higher than 10 ft.

STORAGE CAN BE HIDDEN The best way to hide storage is to make it three-dimensional in deep spaces that can be accessed by one door, à la the walk-in closet. This approach harbors far more items per cubic foot than standard single-hinge deep closets. The philosophy of the walk-in closet, the great spatial liberator and door reducer born in the 1960s, should apply to all things stored: food, toys, hobby items, and so on. If your present home is storage challenged, you may be able to create more storage in fewer square feet if you think about fully packing the available space.

WHERE TO PUT THE STAIRS If you are thinking of adding a floor or just relocating an unsafe staircase, be aware that stairs can be placed anywhere, but it's a question of cost. When a new staircase fully interrupts a home's basic structural system, the entire floor around it has to be resupported and that support needs to be brought all the way down to Mother Earth. Beyond cost concerns, stairs should never get in front of a view and should never be a long distance from where you enter your home most frequently. It is almost mandatory that you hire a design pro if you are contemplating a staircase addition or relocation because it involves safety and code issues as well as restructuring.

BELOW: Even the smallest closet benefits from careful subdivision and the use of built-ins for storage.

before & AFTER

A center stairway in a small suburban house of many levels felt like a cattle shoot with its side walls sealed up and its narrow handrail difficult to grip. Fortunately, the stairs themselves had closed stringers, which made it possible to replace the existing side walls and rail with an open handrail and balusters using painted wood, cherry, and steel. The stair's opened sides bring light down from an existing skylight through three levels of the house.

One side benefit of stairs is that they are a story-and-a-half or two-story space even in the smallest of homes so they are the greatest venting element of your house. Use skylights or clerestory windows at the top of the stairs to minimize air-conditioning and maximize comfort when it gets sticky.

HALLWAYS CAN BE MORE THAN PASSAGEWAYS

Hallways in most stock plans are invariably depressing, with openings limited to bedrooms, a linen closet, and a bathroom with all the ambiance of institutional efficiency. These rude access sluices often have no natural light, and a code-mandated minimum width allows only one person at a time to walk down them. But there are ways to make hallways less depressing without breaking the bank.

If the doors going into two or three bedrooms are close together, consider making an alcove, recessing the doors to break the hall's unrelenting line. If there is a roof overhead, a skylight can alleviate the feeling of depression. If you can handle a little bit of sound sharing, transoms above doors bring natural light to the hall where skylights are impossible. And if in your remodel you can make a doorway or window at the end of the hall open to the outside world, the hallway becomes a passage to the Promised Land.

Even if you can't afford these renovations, more lighting in a typical hallway makes it less depressing, especially if it is focused on artwork hung along its way. Greater color variation in terms of the ceiling or above the heads of the doors helps too, as does adding a trim line at waist level (a chair rail) or connecting the top of the doors. Giving the doors themselves special treatment (natural

ABOVE: A window at the end of a passageway is a more pleasing option than a blank wall.

There are ways to make hallways less depressing without breaking the bank.

before & **AFTER**

Taking out a wall between the hallway and the kitchen made it possible to add built-ins in the opened-up space to greatly increase the amount of storage. Exisiting doors, floors, and most other walls were kept intact, thereby saving money.

wood, differentiated color, and so on) can make a hallway a pleasant transition rather than a mean forced march.

A ROOM SHOULD NOT BE A HALLWAY While it is okay to walk through some rooms to get to other rooms (small offices, perhaps a den on the way to the master bedroom), for the most part rooms that act as passageways ruin the room that is the passageway. If you can limit the path through the room to one end, then the damage is minimal. On the other hand, if you enter on one corner and have to walk diagonally across to the other corner to get to where you are going, you need to seriously rethink the flow of your house. Similarly, if the room itself has a large piece of furniture in its space (a dining room table, sectional sofa) and you must turn right corners to avoid it when getting from point A to point B, a redesign can avoid chronic hip

bruises. This is the type of problem an architect or designer can attack with a perspective you can't be expected to have.

Your walls and columns

There are really only two types of walls: walls that hold things up and walls that simply separate two spaces in your house set between floors or roof structure that are completely supported elsewhere. The walls that set like curtains are called nonbearing partitions and can be moved at will for a reasonable cost. The other walls (basically, all exterior walls and probably a quarter to a half of the rest of the interior partitions) and virtually all columns are bearing (unless your home is a stage set for a Greek drama). Before you assume you can remake your home's interior, consider the following facts about what's what inside.

ABOVE: Columns open up space at less expense than using long, unsupported beams. In this remodel, a wall was removed and the new column (right) mimics an existing one (left) to provide a better connection between the kitchen and informal living space.

- Moving or changing bearing walls or columns can be quite expensive and problematic because these elements need full support all the way down to the ground. A builder, engineer, or architect must weigh in about where the bearing walls are in your house before you think about choreographing how your house's interior will be modified.

- Every wall in your house has only one prime directive—to stay vertical. What works against this vertical condition (what carpenters call plumb) is a lack of stability at the top or bottom of the wall. It's easier for walls higher than 12 ft. to stop being vertical simply because the higher the wall extends, the more likely it is to bend (the engineer's term is *deflect*) in response to things like wind or simple loads that come more from one side than another.

....

- Often walls stop being vertical because people have chopped out connections to the floors they are attached to. This can happen when a staircase is retrofit, when a ceiling is removed to make a cathedralized space, or when what the wall sits on (called the sill plate, which sits on top of the foundation wall) rots and things begin to shift (see "Settlement" on p. 33).

....

- Walls that are out of plumb (not set 90 degrees to your floor and ceiling) need to be either stabilized or made plumb. Stabilization can be relatively easy. Once any rot is removed, metal angles and clips can be used to stabilize the connection to the floor above or the floor below. If the condition is too active and the wall is too far out of plumb, you may need to replace the wall and put in a new one that is perpendicular to the rest of the framing (this is not cheap).

....

- Walls are weakened when they have holes cut in them for doors and windows; often you can see diagonal cracking from these openings up to the ceiling or down to the floor. When that weakened condition is overloaded or the house around the opening has shifted due to settling or inadequacies of the existing framing, cracks will appear over time.

ABOVE: Curves and columns allow you to conceal structure in an artful way that belies their prosaic and structural necessity.

It's probably not a good idea to remove the skin over your walls without understanding the dangers of what's behind them.

what's behind the walls can come out to bite your budget

Homes are inherently obvious and yet totally opaque. They're obvious because everybody lives in one, and they're made of stuff that all of us have seen our entire lives (walls, windows, roofs). But they're also literally opaque. Most people have no idea what is under the top coat of paint that surrounds them and usually live in terror of wires, pipes, heating ducts, and other mysteries. Truth is the innards of your home are like the innards of any machine, say your car's engine. They're made by man, assembled by man, and ultimately can be reworked by man. But it all comes down to cost.

Opening up walls to see what's inside them reveals a couple of things:

• Things that go between floors like forced-air ducting, staircases, and waste lines (the pipes that actually use gravity to take the after effects of washing and personal hygiene out of your house); these are expensive to move.

• Things that contain stuff under pressure (hot and cold running water, electricity, the heated water that's used for your radiators); these can be moved quite easily.

The structure of your home accommodates two types of forces that affect every building: gravity (holding things up) and the loads that wind and earthquakes put on our homes (the sideways forces). Gravity can be accommodated by beams that redirect the weight of your structure and the things that sit on it down into the ground by your foundation under your home. The stuff that protects your home from the shakes involves stiffening elements so that parts of your home are quite rigid. Accommodating changes that affect these realities can get pricey.

So if you want to do a little selective demo, it's a good idea to talk to a builder about where it's safe to actually see what's behind a wall you're interested in moving.

If you are thinking about restructuring, you should be well aware that it involves more than redecorating. It must be done right and involves a fair amount of thought and often cash. Make sure the cost of fixing is worth the investment *before* you launch into the construction.

Your floors

It may surprise you that fixing sagging or bouncy floors is relatively low risk compared to repairing the other parts of your house. It is remarkably easy to spot a floor that's in trouble through the presence of cracks in the ceiling below it. Think of your floors as drumskins: They vibrate. When properly designed, they vibrate a little but not enough to make the material that's below the floor (plaster or drywall) crack. If the ceiling below the floor is paneled, it will hide any evidence of deflection. But there is a second simple way to find out if your floors are not holding their own: Jump on them—if *you* move a lot, it's time to get a pro in

BELOW: New floors can visually unify the entire interior of a house that used to be split into separate rooms.

to see if the cost of repair is worth it. Another clue is the movement in a floor as somebody else walks across it and you're standing still. If the movement the walker causes feels like a vibration, then that floor is probably just fine. If that movement feels as if you were on a trampoline, it's time to bring in a builder, architect, or engineer.

Stiffening up a floor is one of the easier construction tasks, accomplished either by adding a new beam to support the floor's long span into two shorter ones or "sistering" the existing floor structure. Sistering means laminating each one of the floor joists with a second new piece of framing lumber. Sistering is hard to price if there's a lot of plumbing, wiring, or ducts under the floor, and putting new beams into the floor cavity is also potentially expensive.

Your roof

Before you decide to spend your life's saving on a remodel, make sure the fundamentals (like any roof problems) can be fixed and still leave money to hit your other needs. Chronic roof leaks are more often due to the shape of the roof rather than a failure of the materials that were used to make it watertight. When roofs pitch into things (chimneys or dormers), collected rainwater hits the joint hard, and its pressure is almost never defeated by flashing, especially when snow and ice make things worse. If you have these geometric conditions, it's a good idea to rethink your roof's shape rather than keep throwing money at new and more ugly expansions and extensions of your flashing.

OVERHANGS/EAVES The vast majority of homes built over the last couple of generations were built for profit, which typically means a minimal overhang on a roof beyond an applied gutter. Eaves cost money to create, and gutters are designed to look like eaves (kinda).

However, eaves are the miracle drug when it comes to the long-term life of your home. They are omega fatty acids, anti-oxidants, and miracle cold cream combined. That fountain of youth is more expensive to retrofit than to build new but may be worth it. Eaveless homes need more frequent caulking, painting, and window maintenance, and they overheat in the summer, stressing out your A/C system (and your bank account). You need to decide if you have money to spend on eaves creation as you think about your budget.

ROOFING America's default roofing and reroofing material—asphalt shingles—is typically the tried-and-true, best bang for the buck. When installed correctly, wood roofs should last two or three times as long as an asphalt roof (and cost two or three times more), though they have a greater volatility of lifespan depending on their exposure to the sun, tree overhangs, and so on. Metal roofs last longer than wood roofs but cost more money. Slate and tile roofs last forever and consequently cost more money.

ABOVE: Big window walls need deep eaves to provide long-term protection from the elements, especially when facing south (as here) to prevent overheating in summer.

Roofing is easily budgetable by professionals. Get all the options and make sure you understand all the implications as the top of your house should be the bottom line when it comes to investing in your long-term occupancy.

VENTING Obviously, the lighter the color of the roof's surface, the less heat will build up in your attic, but the traditional logic is that you want to keep the air below

ABOVE: Attics not only need to be insulated against unwanted heat loss in winter and unwanted heat gain in summer, but they also need to be carefully vented to the eaves that surround them and to the roof peaks to allow for full airflow.

your roof the same temperature as the ambient air outside to prevent condensation. Unless the roof is well vented with low openings for make-up air at the eaves and outflow at the peak, venting doesn't do a whole heck of a lot. Creating venting is easy and cheap, but it means the floor of your attic needs real insulation and a vapor barrier, so vet out all the implications with a pro.

There are also those who think that it is best to have a fully sealed, fully insulated cavity rather than any void vented above your ceiling, and the science is evolving. Take the time to listen to competing purveyors of different approaches.

Floor-to-floor elements

In thinking about remodeling your house, anything that is isolated to any given floor (like any room interior) is far easier to price, conceptualize, and execute than the things that have to go from the bottom of your house to the top of your house, such as stairs or structure, HVAC systems, or plumbing. These elements can be very expensive to rectify if deficient or dangerous and can often make a potential renovation project simply unfeasible, so vet out their viability before you launch.

DO YOUR STAIRS MEET CODE? If your stairs seem questionable to you, they probably are. The most obvious problem is when the stair riser (the vertical part) changes dimension in one run of the steps, which can cause a major trip. Usually this happens at the top or bottom of a stair run when stock stairs are dropped into a custom setting or somebody has layered up the floor at the top or bottom of the run to the point at which you have more than a ½-in. discrepancy between that riser and all the other risers in the stair.

If your barrier rails (the nonangled straight ones) are lower than 3 ft., they don't meet code. If your hand rails are not continually accessible from the very bottom of the stairs to the very top of the stairs (and if they don't actually return into the wall), they probably don't meet code either. If you have a Certificate of Occupancy for your house and your stairs do not meet code, the only liability you have is if somebody trips and falls and sues you. Truth be told it is a good idea to make your stairs work, not for liability or for code issues, but because you want your house to be safe.

You need an architect to help you with staircase renovation.

insulation 101

If your home has not been renovated in the last 40 years, there's a good chance that it is underinsulated. The roof loses the lion's share of heat in the winter and generates the most unwanted heat in the summer, so the insulation approach at the top of your house needs to have the most money and thought applied to it to save you the most money in the long run.

Most homes today are still insulated with fiberglass. Although it is an irritant, when fiberglass is completely sealed within a wall or ceiling cavity it is pretty benign. Most people don't know there are two types of fiberglass insulation. Standard issue is very adequate to insulate for most climates at a low cost. But there is also a high-performance version with a tighter weave, which provides enhanced performance and allows existing homes with smaller cavities to retrofit at a higher R-value at a modestly higher cost.

There are any number of foam products, all better insulators and more expensive than fiberglass; and if they fill a roof cavity fully, venting ceases to be an issue. Cellulose, recycled newspaper, and any number of green alternatives exist, but the seminal decision is whether your wall or ceiling surfaces need to be removed to get a level of energy efficiency that justifies the huge pain and cost that gut rehab inflicts. It all comes down to cost: If the pros prove you can pay for the new insulation in energy savings, it's probably worth it, but they should do the math and give you options.

before & **AFTER**

In a remodel of a 1920s coastal home, a tight, unsafe existing staircase was replaced by a new staircase that had its run reversed to provide a gentler climb. The use of color and natural wood as well as decorative newels transformed a functional necessity into an architectural feature within the home.

Builders may fake it, and stair builders may claim to be experts, but both have a vested interest in spending your money and a limited desire to create beauty. An architect wants to keep his or her license and will give you the straight skinny on what you can and can't do—and we like making things look good. Replacing or rebuilding stairs can be enormously expensive so everything needs to be priced. You use stairs every day; they usually end up in the middle of your house; they might as well not kill you, jamb your fingers, or look like a hot-glued kit-of-parts assembly.

CHIMNEYS Old chimneys (those built before World War II) are probably not safe unless their flues have been relined. Gaps can happen between stone or brick, and the out-gassing from fireplaces is potentially life-threatening (especially if your home has been completely sealed up tight as a drum with new insulation). However, watch out for putative chimney sweep/re-flue artists who go around presenting worse-case scenarios; vet out at least three competitors and review their proposals with a builder and/or a design pro before proceeding.

PLUMBING In terms of things that go from the lowest level of your house to the highest level, plumbing is a double-edged sword. Supply pipes, the thin lines that actually push water (cold and hot) to where you want it to go, are easily moved anywhere you like as long as you avoid situations where they might freeze up (on outside walls) and provide shutoffs that are accessible to deal with any future leaks that might happen.

It's the waste lines that need gravity to work that become problematic when dealing with floor-to-floor renovations. These pipes are big, and they weaken any piece of structure they have to be cut through to maintain their flow to your septic or sewer system. In rare conditions you can actually macerate and pressurize solid waste to push it through smaller pipes without the aid of gravity, but trusting a pump to evacuate your poop is not only somewhat risky but also costly.

HEATING AND COOLING SYSTEMS Air temperature is one area where you have far more control than you might think. A good builder or architect can give you a general overview of your options but you probably know where your existing system does and doesn't work (which rooms are too hot or too cold, where pipes have frozen, and so on). If the heating plant itself is older than 30 years, there is a high probability that it needs to go—though older boilers can actually be made fairly efficient given the retrofit of new technology.

hvac rules of thumb

Heating, venting, and air-conditioning systems come in many varieties, but essentially they either push treated water (heated or cooled) to blowers that transfer that heated or cooled medium to the air itself or take heated water to radiators (almost always on perimeter walls) that provide heating.

The real issue in thinking about the heating and cooling systems in a home renovation is the parts that weave through the walls and floors—either pipes or ducts. If you have or want a forced-air system, the ducts (returns) that bring your home's air back to the source of its treatment can be quite huge and problematic to retrofit given the nature of most older homes and structures that involve bearing walls and ceilings that may already be too low. But clever builders, architects, and HVAC suppliers typically have many options to choose from. One of the best times to think about finalizing the HVAC approach is after demolition has begun so you can get sound cost estimates for the likely options. This perspective can help you see how the heating and cooling system may affect your floor plan—and make the system cheaper to install and easier on the eye in terms of all the fur-downs and fur-outs of ceilings and wall areas.

- The more zones your house has for heating and cooling, the cheaper it will be in the long run.

- The higher up the cooled air comes out of a wall (or better from the ceiling), the more effectively it cools the space.

- The lower and closer to the perimeter of your home the heated air comes from, the more efficiently your system functions.

- The shorter the distance the heated or cooled air or water travels to get to the rooms it serves, the less energy is used.

- The higher up the returns are (top of the stairs, second floor), the more effectively they bring back air to be retreated with less energy use.

There is nothing wrong with putting a bunch of capable subcontractors into a competition for your dollar and picking their brains and expertise for the approach that seems to make the most sense to you. As long as you've got a builder or architect to vet out what the positive and negative implications of each approach are, you are empowered to make the right choices.

2

Make it happen

Remodeling requires a variety of approvals and pragmatic evaluations to see if the work is feasible or makes sense.

Once you've evaluated your house and determined that a remodel makes sense functionally and financially,

you need to get down to practical matters: dealing with the building department, hiring an architect, selecting a builder, and so on. No designer, builder, or government can understand how you live well enough to tell you how your home should work, but you do need an objective frame of reference to understand what the experts know that falls outside of your experience. In this chapter, we'll look at some ways to gain that knowledge. Just like anyone going into rehab, acknowledging that your home does not work for you is the first step. Once you own that fact, action is required. This book is a window to the risks and rewards of reforming a home that you hate without breaking your bank or, more important, your spirit.

Dealing with the building department

There are many benefits to remodeling (versus wholesale adding on or building new), but the window for grandfathering in any aspects of your present home that do not conform to existing laws or regulations is dwindling. Effectively, in most municipalities when you file for a building permit that involves doing work on a new non-code-compliant part of your home, Grandpa has left the building. The minute you file for a building permit, you need to get real with what meets the regulations now. What follows are things you need to think about before jumping in.

Just like anyone going into rehab, acknowledging that your home does not work for you is the first step.

1. Site survey. You need an accurate survey of your property, especially if the remodel will affect the footprint of your home in any way. There may be a survey on file at the town hall—if there is, you will save money, even if it needs updating. New surveys cost between $1,000 and $5,000, depending on where you live and the conditions of your property. It is a very reasonable, often necessary, investment to put the characteristics of your site on paper. The more expensive surveys will give you the location of your existing

before & AFTER

In a neighborhood with extremely tight zoning, the only way to avoid a time-consuming variance for this Cape remodel was to build a new second floor within the setbacks.

septic system, the trees around your home, and the actual contour/grading of your lot. At the very least, you need to locate your house within the property lines and find out whether things like wetlands, zoning setbacks, or your septic system present problems.

2. Zoning issues. Unless somebody made a huge mistake before you owned your home or you simply went ahead and expanded the footprint without asking anybody's permission, pretty much everything that you have now is grandfathered into code acceptance if not compliance. The vast majority of homes built in tight communities before zoning laws were imposed have some aspect that is in technical violation of what the rules are now—these homes are typically set too close to their property lines or are too big for their site. But that was then and this is now, and you can have what you have—unless you are proposing to increase the size of your house. With a survey in hand, it's pretty easy for you to go to your town's or county's zoning enforcement officer (in larger towns they have several of those) and simply get an overview of what district you are in and what the limitations are.

know the code

Beyond getting clear on your specific needs, building anything in 21st-century America means it's necessary to have an understanding of what your state, county, and town imposes on construction projects—so find out where the zoning code is on file (and/or online) and get to know its labyrinth up close and personal. The Internet is the first place to start, but a phone call will provide a reality check of who you need to talk to.

Playing dumb helps more than being aggressive. Be sweet, complimentary, and quick to laugh at the gallows humor that most of these professionals offer up (remember most of their life is spent raining on other people's parades).

....

3. If it's wet. If your home is located on the coast or next to a lake, swamp, or stream, you'll need to see somebody called a wetlands officer and/or the town engineer because there are often state, county, and federal regulations that have extreme impact not only on what you can do but also on how you do it. These regulations are extraordinarily byzantine, often draconian, and involve huge amounts of time even when you play by the rules.

Before you jump into a remodeling project, find the one local attorney who deals with the town the most.

4. Get legal. Depending on what you found out when you went to Town Hall with an accurate survey, if you need to address any of the laws that regulate what you can and can't build, it is probably a good idea to find the best local land-use attorney. This will cost some money, but that money can be greatly limited if you frame the question tightly by talking to all of the players involved at Town Hall—zoning enforcement officer, town engineer, wetland officer, and so on—*before* you hire the lawyer. Reputation and experience are far more important than personality or a personal

what do we mean by building height?

The most variable thing in all zoning codes is height interpretation. If you are adding on to your existing home vertically, you need to make sure that, if possible, you don't need to go for a variance. The variables in determining height between different towns, counties, and states are enormous and include the determination of what level of dirt applies as the baseline for your work (it is either the grade when you are done or the grade when you've begun). How that grade is determined is either from the highest point, the lowest point, or an average between the highest point and the lowest point, and that level is to the highest allowable roof level. It might be the peak, the mean roof height averaging eaves and peaks, or an averaging of all the eaves to roof peak heights—or yet another methodology! Unlike law or medicine, the specifics of these regulations are intended for public use—not to pad a lawyer's billings. Press the town official to define anything you are not clear on.

connection with an attorney. Your brother-in-law might be a great guy, but if he deals with trusts and estates he will have just about the same amount of knowledge base as you do in dealing with the town. Before you jump into a remodeling project, find the one local attorney who deals with the town the most. He or she will know what the opportunities are and what the bottom line really is in a sea of ambiguity.

5. Architects can be helpful. Just like lawyers, the brother-in-law architect who designs shopping malls in Indiana is not the one you want to talk to if you want to remodel a kitchen in a flood plain. Look for an architect who's had some experience with remodels, especially one who has worked in your town.

6. Going it alone. If you decide to take charge of your project's code compliance (in other words, if you want to save some money and time and take on the burden of zoning, septic, and engineering issues yourself), the best thing you can do is spend some time going through the "definitions" section of your town's various codes. Almost all the zoning codes are now available online and can be accessed 24 hours a day. The vast majority of misconceptions in zoning codes, septic codes, and other codes have to do with how you interpret the words that are used. Terms like *encumbrance, variance,* and *building height*

Focusing where you build makes projects more affordable. Here, an existing porch was kept, as was the general location of the front door (lower left), but the existing roof was replaced to create attic space.

are somewhat terrifying until you actually spend the time to learn the language. Armed with that knowledge, you can patiently walk through the various departments and figure out the path you want to take. It will take time and patience.

Working with the pros

It's tough for an architect to admit it, but the vast majority of home remodeling projects are executed "without the advice of counsel"—with no money spent to hire architects, landscape architects, interior designers, or garden designers. Most home renovation projects are elaborated repair work with the occasional removed wall or dropped-in window.

You don't need a professional designer to tell you what room to paint if you already hate the color. But most of us who live in a house we did not have a hand in designing want to do more than that. Professional advice in dealing with your most significant asset and risk makes a lot of sense on a variety of levels, and there are ways you can maximize the benefits of working with any professional designer.

Words have power

Any profession, whether lawyer, doctor, or Indian chief, has its own lingo. In terms of remodeling, it might be a builder talking about "unforeseen conditions" or an architect pontificating on "hierarchical forms." The more you can cut through the baloney the better. You probably can't make somebody who has been doing something his or her entire life give up the language that they think in, but you can be your own translator. It is probably a good idea (if you haven't already) to tune into as many DIY shows as possible, subscribe to magazines like *Fine Homebuilding,* and simply talk to as many people as you can about what actually happens during a remodeling project vs. what the self-serving verbal smokescreens are from those who you are dealing with.

The contract is the key

Most people don't understand that when you get drawings from a designer (whether an architect, unlicensed home designer, or interior designer) those drawings should be a part of your contract. In home remodeling, most people go directly to a builder first, who takes charge and gets the drawings done. The builder will hire somebody who will never see you or listen to you, and who will draw what the builder wants drawn (because he or she is paying them) and produce something that may or may not work. The rationalization for this is that the drafting fees are buried in the cost of construction. Those fees might be as low as $500, but for a large renovation they might end up as much as $5,000.

If you opt to hire your own designer, you have two options: a designer or an architect with a license. Hiring an architect will probably cost more but he or she usually has a broader knowledge base. A typical architect's fee for a remodel may go from 6 percent of your project budget all the way up to 15 percent or more; designers usually charge less depending on who you hire and what the scope of the work is.

As to the unlicensed design consultants that you might hire, the work they produce is extraordinarily varied. You can get the best services available down through something similar to the draftsman that a builder would provide. There are two benefits to paying more for somebody at the higher end of the skill range.

BELOW: A new in-law apartment (right) helped create a sheltered walkout terrace that virtually doubled the living space for Mom and Dad.

If that person is doing what he or she should be, you will have far more options presented to you and a greater level of care taken in the actual execution of the conceptual design before construction. Second, the drawings that are generated by a seasoned pro you hire independently keep a builder honest. The drawings he or she produces should have a level of specification and control that prevents builders from coming back for add-ons and unforeseen costs.

Bidding is a good thing

Once you've decided you want to hire a design professional directly (vs. a builder who will then hire drafting help), it never hurts to put the job out to bid. There are several ways to bid: fixed price, time and materials capped with a maximum cost cap, or a nonbinding estimate with the final cost level based on what time is spent and what materials are brought. My own personal approach is to get a nonbinding cost estimate based on a sketch design from at least three builders as soon as possible in the design process so the costs involved in paying the design professional are limited and an economic reality check is given to the project as early as possible.

To state the obvious, the lowest bidder is not always the best builder. In the process, you'll get a sense of who is taking the bidding seriously and who has the most cogent

Beware of the foot-in-the-door low-ball bid.

do your homework

You know more than anyone about your house, and you can define what's wrong in several ways that are easily communicable to a professional designer. Easiest to determine are the things that drive you crazy. Living in an existing home that does not work for you is an effective litmus test for what you actually want. What you hate directly affects what you will love.

• First, make a prioritized list of what you want your remodel to accomplish.

• Next, find images in magazines or your own photographs of places you see around you that send you into flights of desire or are so antithetical to your values that they make you laugh in headshaking amusement (yes, the bad and the ugly can be as effective as the good in communicating your desires to an architect or designer).

• Then take the bull by the horns and simply draw out your home the way it appears to you in a floor plan. This is best done over a hard-line to-scale plan of your existing house; if you don't have one, it's worth the $500 to $1,000 to have a pro provide one for you. Your work doesn't have to be even close to accurate; it's just a diagram. Draw on that plan the things that your list conveys (both the things you hate and the things you would love to have) in the context of your four walls—and perhaps where your four walls simply can't contain them and demand some form of expansion.

These acts of description accelerate the discernment and insights your designer desperately needs from you, and they save time and should save money spent on design fees if you raise the bargaining chip before you sign a contract.

But the greatest gift of defining your discomfort is that it will give you hope. It is too easy to simply curse the darkness and walk away from a problematic house. It is actually a lot more productive (and fun) to create a scenario where you can see light at the end of the tunnel of your domestic despair and take action.

insights into the drawings that they receive. But typically the highest bidders are throwing money at the project in hopes that they can avoid a financial crunch if things go awry.

During boom times, builders are far less likely to bid and advocate just estimating and doing work on a pay-what-is-billed basis. One of the upsides for the homeowner of bidding during a weak market is that builders are now much more willing to bid and much more interested in bidding accurately. Conversely, beware of the foot-in-the-door low-ball bid. If most builders have clearly priced your project higher and one builder has priced much lower than all the others (especially for the foundation, framing, and plumbing parts of the project), something is probably wrong.

Selecting a builder

"Past is prologue" accurately reflects the basis on which you should hire a builder. Rather than look at the ads in your local *Pennysaver*, canvas all your friends (and then indirectly their friends) to get a list of builders who have worked well on similar projects before. Meet the candidates in person and look at the work they have done.

If you have hired a pro to design your project before you hire a builder, that architect or designer will have a list of builders he or she has worked with. If that designer or architect has a "sweetheart" relationship with the builder, be wary of it. "You rub my back, I'll rub yours" always means you are the one who foots the bill. If there is never any responsibility for *any* problem other

before &
AFTER

A simple infill addition (center) and a small extension (far left) bring the deck and garage space into the heated finished area of a small Ranch house.

than you paying for it, something is wrong. Architects make mistakes and so do builders. If they have worked together for years, they may want to pretend that no one ever makes a mistake. The honesty that happens when independent professionals contract directly with you means you get the benefit of each professional's insight about the other's work.

The contract itself

In any remodel or small addition project, there will always be things that are unknowable; therefore, no matter how you slice it, it is a great idea to have at least 20 percent of your budget as mad money—a number beyond the contract price. This might cover fixing the surprise rot in your walls or being able to have a feature you are madly in love with if the project runs smoothly.

In any remodeling project, it pays to have a 20 percent funding cushion.

You can either start with a fixed cost based on drawings and specs or you can trust the builder to bill you for costs (plus a fee) as they come due. Neither is perfect because a fixed price may be padded to protect the builder and a cost-plus or time-and-materials contract may have no limits. Once a dollar amount is determined as a reasonable budget for the project, I think it is generally best to have a fixed-fee contract. When builders say that it works to your benefit to have a cost-plus agreement, that may be true if everything works out perfectly, but

Mudrooms are often leftover spaces—drab corners for storage, laundry, or garden prep. This light-filled mudroom space between a house and a garage was completed reinvented to accommodate multiple functions.

the truth is there is no motivation and no incentive to do things efficiently, economically, and on time if there is an open-ended availability of funds.

Some people think a fixed-fee contract shows a lack of respect for a builder's integrity but I think the reverse is true. It says the builder is professional and is bidding to the point at which he or she will not get hurt. Almost all disagreements after a contract has been signed have to do with something the pros call "scope of work"—defining what the complete finished job is. Good drawings preempt that. Poor drawings (especially drawings done at the builder's behest) facilitate ambiguity and therefore give the builder a great deal of latitude in saying "I never had that in my bid."

Similarly, homeowners can assume there may be things in a contract that aren't actually stated in it. For example, a homeowner may assume the entire house will be painted in a remodeling. But the builder can honestly believe he or she contracted to paint only the area that was remodeled—unless the specs are written into the contract. This is yet another reason why hiring an independent pro to design your renovation addition is helpful. Such professionals should have the integrity to mediate these disputes and decide what is fair and what is not. Typically they don't have a dog in the hunt. They are thinking about the next 30 or 40 jobs they will work on, not just yours, and therefore will be fair to a skilled builder that they would like to work with again and to you, who is a source of referrals for now and forever.

Typically, the most efficient way to handle any project is one-stop shopping with a GC.

Job organization

There are typically two ways to organize any construction job. You can either have a general contractor (GC) who will execute everything under one umbrella contract, or you can split things up so the GC does the nuts and bolts and you get separate contracts from a variety of tradespeople, including a landscaper, a painter, and the professionals who perform the finishing touches (for example, millwork, flooring, painting, and window treatments).

ABOVE: Widening an existing opening and carefully integrating appliances make a new kitchen for a 19th-century home function without compromise.

The danger with the second scenario is that the more contracts you have, the more things fall through the cracks—or you might be double-billed when the GC assumes he or she is handling something and the interior designer or subcontractors assume they are handling the same thing. Typically, the most efficient way to handle any project is one-stop shopping with a GC, but there are some ways you can save a GC's fee at relatively low risk.

1. Painting. The builder is just about done when the painters come onboard, and you can independently bid and control that service. It does mean that you have less leverage over the builder, because the more money that is hanging out there, the more impetus there is to get everything wrapped up in a timely fashion, but the risk is minimal.

find your home: the bungalow

Originating in 19th-century India (as in Bengal), the Bungalow has become as American as apple pie and is virtually a Cape with a porch and a dominant roof. Our version was born at the start of the 20th century, and took the Cape, applied Arts and Crafts style, and moved the chimney (absurd in India's climate) that clogged the center of the Cape to the gable end of the house, thereby freeing up the interior. Not unlike Frank Lloyd Wright's Usonian houses, the Bungalow was seen as a way to get many people into nice houses quickly and cheaply.

The Bungalow's interiors have a variety of room sizes as the structure is as basic as the Cape's. Just like the Cape, the second floors are often restricted by the original roof size, but unlike the Cape, there is often a second floor designed into the roofscape featuring large central shed dormers, gable-faced dormers, or multiple versions thereof.

One aspect of Bungalows that is unlike the Cape, Federal, or Colonial is that it isn't inherently bland in coloration. Rather than cloaked in an all-white, generic shingles or clapboards, a Bungalow can be "of color." Because of its origins in the Arts and Crafts movement, the Bungalow celebrates rich material differences between different types of wood, uses color explosions, and has the self-defining freedom to have large expanses of glass and a variety of window forms.

2. Millwork and cabinetry. Finish work happens at the very end of a cycle of construction but does integrate with the electrician and plumber. If you opt to go with an independent bid for the millwork and cabinetry, remember that you need to have a meeting with the builder and the supplier to get everything coordinated. Sometimes the designer you hired has the capacity to bid your millwork out to shops that he or she has worked with in the past, and this gives you the benefit of bidding and not having the fee of the builder applied to the millwork supplied.

3. Purchasing pieces and parts. The ability to buy your own light fixtures, plumbing supplies, and door hardware can save you a fair amount of money, but be aware that it has to be very carefully stipulated in the contract to make sure there's no double billing. You also need to make certain that contractually the obligation is very clear that, although you are supplying given products, the professionals have to install them. You also have to be careful that if you have a defective product, someone (not you) takes responsibility for it—preferably your supplier.

Phasing

You don't have to remodel everything all at once, even if you intend to have the result look and function as if you had. There is never enough money to do everything, and if you are staying in the house during the full remodel, there is never enough space to sequester yourself if you try to do everything at the same time. So if you do not have the cash for the full Monty, or if you worry about paying for the rental of a second home during construction, there are several ways to phase. The following are some of the most common.

1. Start big. Do the broadest part of the project first (this usually means exterior construction and large-scale demolition) and save the least important finishing to the last. If you add a second-floor space but only need part of it now, frame it all and leave the future-use part interior unfinished. If you don't cook that much, perhaps the kitchen can be the last phase (the reverse is also true: If you love to cook, the kitchen should be the first phase). If you work out of your home, then the home office has to rule the roost because it generates income; if not, it can wait. Most people can accept a not-so-great bedroom, so that often pulls up the rear.

2. Phase for living comfortably. If your phased project leaves an unfinished space that you walk through every day, it'll frustrate the heck out of you until it's finished. Try to figure out a way to make a workable complete house now, with the areas that are temporarily unfinished being out of sight, out of mind.

3. Be safe. Construction is toxic to children. Remember that living in a construction site with preadolescent children is inherently dangerous. You either have to fully seal off any of the areas where construction is occurring or simply move out until the work is done. (This is not about stepping on nails. It's about breathing in particulates and chemicals that can damage growing lung tissue.)

4. Work the budget. Don't just think about the money you have available now. Think about the money you hope you'll have in the future and edit the master plan accordingly. While it's a mistake to think that you're going to have infinite funds 10 years from now to execute some

how to live through a remodel

Nothing is more predictably unpredictable than the impositions that construction has on a family's quality of life. It can also be hazardous to your health. Here's a perspective you can use before all hell breaks loose.

• Learn to laugh at the things you can't control. Things will go wrong. Pipes will be severed. Power will go out. Food will rot in a refrigerator that doesn't have power. Rainwater will come in and saturate one part of your house. All of these things suck. But they're also temporary, part of your own little reality TV series that you've imposed upon yourself for the greater good.

• Keep your eyes on the prize. Ultimately what you're doing will make things better, and as each piece falls into place realize that when you're done you're getting what you want (even if you don't want to go through what you have to in order to get it). If you sense that each day's tragedy is a death sentence, think again. Each day's tragedy usually ends with the next day's dawn. Perspective is critical to avoiding despair.

• Be liquid. Make sure that there's an economic buffer; 20 percent is common in remodels to give you the

ABOVE: Multiple exterior refinements brought the outside in to an antique home without changing its original character.

sense that you don't have your financial back to the wall and have to invade the kids' college fund to pay for the rot you encountered. Being conservative with the money you have means that if things work out to the good, you could actually be frivolous with it at the end of the project and buy the light fixture or TV you always wanted.

- Be safe. If you're doing a whole-house renovation, leave the premises! Your presence makes the project take longer and cost more and endangers you and your family members' lives. If you're dealing with a small portion of your home, make sure that the builder knows that you want it completely, totally, and permanently sealed off until it's finished so that you can limit the amount of collateral damage that's imposed upon you by your remodel.

- Plan ahead. The more you take complete control of your possessions before the builders come in and destroy where you've been living, the more you'll feel you're under control. It's also a good excuse to throw out those things that your spouse has been hanging on to that you hate.

- Cook outside. If your kitchen is being renovated during the summer, this may be a necessity.

- Brush up on your etiquette. Renovations often mean that many people have to use one bathroom. It's time to channel your inner Waltons and make sure that everybody's schedule aligns before there's a line at the toilet.

- Plan vacations from renovation. Set aside a little money so that when times get worse you can spontaneously take a weekend off and go to a place to refresh and renew your outlook. There's nothing quite as depressing as a three-month project that's in its seventh month. You need to take measures to avoid depression.

grand design, it's even worse to assume you will be laid off for the next decade. Sit down with your financial planner and get a hard bead on what the realistic expectation of expenditures will be for the life cycle of your master plan project. Edit the final design (as well as the part you're building now) to meet those financial expectations so that you can actually build the project rather than have to abort mid-plan.

ABOVE: The space above a garage is a perfect candidate for a remodel. This vaulted-ceiling room above a two-car garage accommodates a variety of activities.

Greening your remodel

Compared with building new (or even more questionably tearing down an existing building to build new), remodeling a house is the single greenest thing you can do. But it is not enough just to save the building; you need to look at a remodeling as an opportunity to make the existing skin, shell, and shape mesh better with its specific environment and minimize energy usage (heating, cooling, and long-term maintenance). Here are some ways to do that.

1. Be a "swamp Yankee." Frugal swamp Yankees never threw out anything that could be repurposed, it just didn't make sense. "Waste not, want not" was not just a cute saying, it was a way of life—a way that green design should be based on. For example, if the flooring in a room that you are expanding is salvageable, it can be used in a smaller room you are renovating elsewhere—the idea of tossing it is offensive.

Similarly, if you are removing windows or doors that are less than 10 years old, think about reusing them. The downside, of course, is that trying to save a dime, you spend a dollar. It costs money to remove things and always costs money to make them reusable (removing nails, repairing certain elements, and so on). But don't always assume that a completely new system needs to be in place once you have remodeled. A 20-year-old heating system can be upgraded simply by providing a new burner. A water heater can remain in place and a smaller unit can be set closer to the new bathroom or laundry that it directly services. Task your builder to evaluate the septic approach carefully. There are times when an existing septic system can be modified or a small secondary septic system can be put into place versus removing an entire septic system and replacing it with a new one. Just because you are remodeling doesn't mean everything needs to be renovated.

2. Task your pros. Make it known early on both to your designer and to your builder that you would like your project to be as efficient as possible. Let them know that to reuse, reclaim, and renew existing (versus ripping out, throwing away, and building new) is part of your ethic, but only on a cost neutral or net cost savings basis. Being conceptually green and costing you a lot of cold, hard cash means that you are tithing to a religion rather than executing a construction project.

Just because you are remodeling doesn't mean everything needs to be renovated.

3. Consider the compass points. The sun is a beautiful and brutal thing. Beautiful in that it can warm your house in the winter (if you live in a part of the country that has winters) and brutal in that it can overheat and decay any building materials that are put in south light's exposure.

If you are in a temperate climate and would like to get the sun into the house at a given time, any new space you add should be angled to get the right exposure. It also will mean that you put more windows facing south. Obviously that also means that there should be a greater eaves overhang to prevent overheating during the summer. If, alternatively, you live in the South, you need to think about ways in which you can avoid all direct unshielded south light and provide northern exposure to get light into your home but not heat.

4. Vent first, air-condition second. When looking at each individual space in your remodel try to get windows,

skylights, and doors positioned as remotely as possible within the space. It is very easy to have an open window facing the outside but if the breeze is flowing and there is no place for the air to go when it gets into your room, its impact will be almost nil. Think about a skylight in a dead-ended space not only for its backlighting potential but also for its venting capacity. And don't ignore the idea of operable transoms above doors to allow the wind to flow through. Every minute you can keep the air-conditioning off saves money (and is indubitably green).

....

5. Be suspicious of new technologies. New green technologies that are heavily marketed often end up costing far more than they save. *Conceptually* green doesn't always equate to *practically* green—and green washing is nothing new. The 1970s saw millions of solar water heaters tacked onto homes, but most have been ripped off and not replaced simply because the technology did not work.

Similarly, homes that were superinsulated in the 1980s were often so poorly vented that mildew and toxic internal conditions made the home uninhabitable. As photovoltaics, geothermal technologies, and new ways of insulating your house transition from being cutting-edge technologies to viable options with competitive bidding, everything has become more rational. The key is to conduct your own research and to get a minimum of three proposals for any nontraditional element that you are thinking about.

DUO'S DO'S & DON'TS

South is the cruelest compass point

Almost all of us love to have a bright and cheery home. In colder climates, we love the fact that if we orient the long direction of our house facing south, we'll have light and the sun's warmth in the house all day. The unfortunate reality is that every single part of every home is degraded by ultraviolet (UV) exposure. Plastic becomes more brittle, wood actually loses elasticity and flakes away, paint begins to become brittle and powder, and all your interior surfaces (unless you have an anti-UV coating on your windows) begin to bleach out.

Solid inorganic surface materials do fair better. Brick, stone, and stucco are more or less impervious to UV decay. Raw wood will actually have a very long life on three sides of your home but on the south side it will have a very compromised survival rate. And the minute you paint or coat a wood house, the south side will need coating far more often than the other facades. Eaves help defeat this exposure but they don't eliminate it.

3 Kitchen remodels

Getting electrical, gas, water, and air into your kitchen is one thing. Fans also need to be ducted to the outdoors. The surfaces have to be a combination of the bombproof (granite, tile, stainless steel, and the like) and the tactile (wood, softer stone like marble). The handles on your cabinets need to feel good, look good, and be easy to clean.

Kitchen remodels can be complicated.

There is more technology per square foot in your kitchen than in any other part of your house, including your bathroom. Kitchens involve virtually every mechanical system that your house has in a tight do-si-do. Piping snakes water to and from several places. Piping for gas for your stove needs to be safe. The wiring has to be integrated with virtually every part of the design—involving fans, extensive lighting, many outlets, and, of course, all those appliances. Your heat and air-conditioning have to find a way into a tightly designed space that is often open to the rest of your home—not an easy engineering feat.

It is the only room in your house filled with motors— used to compress gas to create cold temperatures for food storage, to allow microwaves to heat, to grind off-cuts in your disposal, and for fans to push the smells out. It's potentially a high-hazard area as well with open flames and electricity in close proximity to water.

It is the only room in your house that is intended to be filled with cabinetry of furniture-grade quality that needs to be extremely durable. The interiors of these cabinets

There is more technology per square foot in your kitchen than in any other part of your house, including your bathroom.

the place of kitchens

The kitchen is the most dramatically changed space in the home since World War II, evolving from a black box of isolated cooking to be the hub of almost every house. It's the new hearth, the social center that also serves as the touchstone of every family's daily ritual of awakening and returning. It deserves the greatest amount of cash, thought, and spatial consideration within any home.

Given these new realities, it's not surprising that kitchens are now taking up the catbird seat in almost every renovation, even when the kitchen itself does not need remodeling— sometimes we renovate the rooms around a viable kitchen to allow the house to live up to it. Kitchen remodeling is the one area of the house that almost always recoups the investment, if done appropriately. It is the one place where thoughtful designers can ethically encourage homeowners to spend a little extra money for custom design and fabrication versus out-of-the-box thinking. Entire books are written about kitchen design, but in this book you will find a simple validation that the kitchen is worth every minute of time you put into planning and every dollar that you commit to its execution.

also have tightly calculated mechanisms for storage of internal appliances, cutlery, food, and so on. The best kitchen remodels, like the ones shown in this book, make all these technical issues disappear by simply being planned into the design *before* construction. Getting cabinetry, all that mechanical equipment, and lighting meshed with your space requires time and money up front for design fees, but the results will be appreciated more than in any other remodeling.

ABOVE: Two spaces were opened up to create one kitchen that kept the original opening. The doubled-up space was split to create cleanup and prep to the left and pastrywork and pantry/oven to the right.

Know your clearances

Given that kitchen remodeling is high-stakes poker (lots of money put in a very small space), the window for devastating miscalculation is wide open. Most people want contradictory results: an efficient, yet open place to cook. A galley layout is very efficient but pretty depressing. So know your clearances and require your designer to pay attention to the way *you* cook. The biggest miscalculations occur in terms of the clearances between all the places you work. Any countertop closer than 36 in. to any other countertop is too tight. Upper cabinets that are less than 12 in. deep can't store large plates. If those cabinets are less than 18 in. off the countertop, they're just too low to let you see what's under them and limit what you can put underneath. Cabinets over new sinks and stoves need to be 24 in. up so you have working room.

Sinks and stoves without set-down spaces on both sides of at least 12 in. (and preferably 24 in.) terminally compromise usefulness (and risk wall damage from hot pots and pans). There can be separation anxiety as well. Any appliance that is more than 6 ft. or 7 ft. from any other appliance makes roller skates a necessity for food preparation.

Design and technology

The myriad complex vulnerabilities of poor kitchen design have generated a lot of effort to rewrite the rules via technological whiz-bangs. Rather than revolutionizing how we use kitchens, many gadgets were revealed to be mostly shallow hype intended to sell. Remember in-countertop mixers? Built-in slide-out toasters? The under-mounted upper cabinet entertainment center that included a tape player, a TV/VCR, and probably a cigarette lighter? How about the bacteria-friendly cutting board that slid out from underneath your countertop? Or the equally distressing sponge trough that popped down from the front of your sink? And who could forget the trash compactor?

Well, today's versions of obsessive integration also try a little too hard. The pricey pasta pot–filling faucet near the stove solves a problem most people didn't know they had. Many kitchens now have an integrated separate under-counter drink refrigerator and a mini under-counter wine cellar as well. There are more digital clocks on appliances than time zones. You deserve everything you want in your kitchen, but most people stop when what they can afford tells them what they really need, so insist on knowing the full breakdown of all costs *before* you pay for any part of your kitchen project.

The pricey pasta pot–filling faucet near the stove solves a problem most people didn't know they had.

Your specific desires all have an effect on the design as a whole. Individual refrigerator drawers, warming ovens, and the swing-up heavy mixer are all set below eye level, complicating storage. Cooktops not only offer different BTUs for each burner but options for variable stovetop grilling and griddling.

Cost control

Beyond these attempts to modernize the process of cooking, the visuals of kitchen design have had enormous mood swings since June Cleaver toiled in a blank room in

make room for prep space

A dedicated prep space is becoming a necessity in today's kitchen. Most of the previous generation's cooking involved at least a partial "boil in bag" mind-set where high-tech replaced loving manual acts of food preparation. Although many of us do use slow cookers, microwave ovens, and other elements that Julia Child might have mocked, the truth is in any given week for a growing number of people, there is a celebratory cooking event that involves multiple materials, a variety of preparation technologies, and manual dexterity and visual focus that are not aided by stock cabinetry, countertop materials, or lighting. To give but one example, more kitchens have stone tops for rolling out pasta and pastry.

isolation. Decorous stone or highly stylized tile surfaces try to make the most high-tech room in your house warm and fuzzy. Alternatively, there are efforts to make everything invisible by flushifying the refrigerator, the dishwasher, and oven, congealing all appliance variations into a homogenized blank "deep wall."

Virtually all of these compensations cost a great deal of money. A simple "letting it all hang out" kitchen design makes things inherently less expensive, allowing various appliances to simply happen. Simple cabinets that are full overlay, where the drawer and door fronts completely box over the cabinet, are usually cheaper and allow you to access more interior space. Having a free-standing stove is cheaper than separate cooktops and ovens. Backsplashes can disappear if covered with laminate or a solid surface material from countertop

BELOW: In this wall-wrapping kitchen, bumping out the window wall allowed room for informal dining at the central island without sacrificing any countertop or storage space.

to upper cabinets or they can be a feature, but probably not worth as much money as your countertop.

Rather than spend as much money on an "altar to venting" shroud for the fan above your cooktop, why not just keep it small and simple? This low-key approach can use standard cabinets and simple durable materials and will always bring costs down. The kitchen renovations shown in this chapter mostly follow a middling ground between techno-denial and artful approach, embracing expressiveness but also cost-effectiveness.

ABOVE: Sometimes it's best to keep everything open. Here, shelves replace upper cabinets and an open steel pot hanger virtually eliminates the boxes that would both clutter walls and obscure the views.

Kitchen connections

If kitchen design were just about cooking, it would be easy. But the kitchen is the one room that needs to connect to every other public room in your house with the greatest amount of ease. Connecting to the mudroom (which in turn connects to the back door or garage) is imperative, given the vast quantities of food and other materials brought in and out on an ongoing basis.

But the new impact in the way kitchens are thought of is in the penumbra of satellite aspects that radiate out from it. The pantry (or sometimes pantries) is mandatory. In addition, more and more kitchens have a place for a second refrigerator and/or freezer in the pantry, garage, or basement.

Large-scale recycling containers are best located as close to the kitchen as possible because many items for recycling are generated there. Further, more people use leftovers as composting material and thus need several recycling containers.

BELOW: In this kitchen remodel, an open flow was achieved by removing two walls, vaulting the ceiling, and extending the existing wood floors.

where are they now?
kitchens as showrooms

Kitchens that had more islands than the Caribbean are resolving themselves into nautical efficiency. People renovating their homes have given up trying to turn kitchens into showrooms that shove cutting-edge technology in your face. It wasn't that long ago that things like microwaves, convection ovens, downdraft ranges, getting cold water from your refrigerator, and even having a disposal were as exciting as an iPad®. Cooking technology has leveled off. The innovations are incremental rather than transformative. Our culture has evolved into loving the act of cooking and exploratory eating rather than feeling akin to the astronauts while baking a potato.

Most people who did not participate in the design of the kitchen they use have real issues with how it works for them. Bad examples are good teachers, but good designers can give you options that you could never think of, and good builders will price those options so you can have control over what you decide to spend money on. And spend you will—and should within reason; it's the place you spend the most time in and closest attention to.

ABOVE: A kitchen involves a fair measure of imposed solitary confinement when you are prepping, cooking, or cleaning up. Since you can't move the sink or the stove once it's installed, you might as well have a view to the outside world, a living space, or the TV.

REMOVING A WALL and applying new countertops are easy to do conceptually, but such work often implies that you need to replace perfectly usable cabinetry, which is not necessarily the case. Half of the kitchen in this small house in a coastal community was perfectly good (with stock cabinets less than 10 years old), but the kitchen itself was closed in by four walls with a small opening to the living and dining areas of the house.

The first step was to double the width of the opening, connecting the place where people like to spend the most time—the kitchen—with the informal living area. Things that are expensive to move (the stove, sink, and window) were left as they were, whereas the refrigerator (easy to move) was transferred from one side to the other. By maintaining all the existing cabinetry and simply replicating that cabinetry with new that more or less matches, and by capping old and new cabinetry with new stone countertops that double the counter surface, the kitchen was completely reinvented without changing half of its contents.

BEFORE

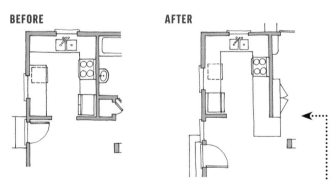

BEFORE   AFTER

The sink and surrounding cabinets are left where they are, while the countertop expands into the living area. The refrigerator is concealed behind the wall of the new framed opening.

Widening the framed opening connects the kitchen with the informal living area. A new entry (right) allows direct access to those coming in from the outside to put down groceries on the newly extended countertop.

The kitchen was completely reinvented without changing half of its contents.

Working with What You've Got

THE ORIGINAL KITCHEN in this 1940s Cape occupied a tight, flat-ceilinged connector between the main house and the garage (a 1970s addition). For the owners, the kitchen was cramped and undersize, with limited storage and no accommodation for the home's back door. The challenge was to get more storage in the same space without adding to the footprint, while keeping the existing window and door location, as well as the original skylight, sink, and flooring, to save money.

Opening up the flat ceiling transformed the space, and the revised layout allowed for far more versatility in cooking, entertaining, and storage. A small laundry–mudroom at one side was slid over to get a closet next to the back door and the door to the garage. The fully filled space was coordinated with a simple, unifying trim and white painted cabinetry. Steel and spaulted-maple appointments, a creative round-the-room light valence, and a new window seat add visual zest to this ensemble.

BEFORE

BEFORE

AFTER

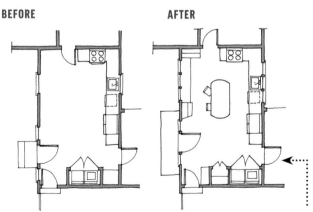

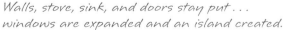
Walls, stove, sink, and doors stay put . . . windows are expanded and an island created.

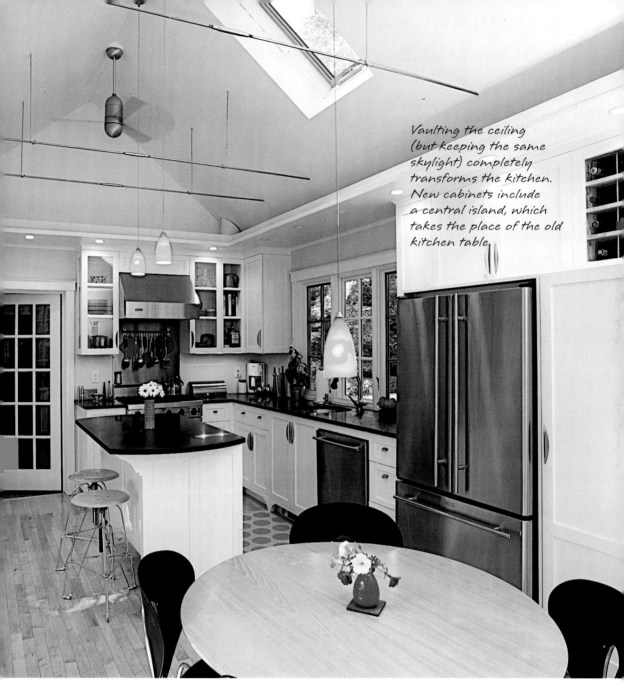

Vaulting the ceiling (but keeping the same skylight) completely transforms the kitchen. New cabinets include a central island, which takes the place of the old kitchen table.

Kitchen remodeling is the one area of the house that **almost always recoups the investment if done appropriately.**

BEFORE

don't move! the value of remodeling around what's there

A great place to start your design is to accept some of the basics: structure, waste-line locations, skylights, and windows. Skylights (like the one in this project) can cost over $2,000 if cut into a new ceiling. Accepting sink locations helps save too. If you can keep kitchen or bath cabinets where they are, the HVAC ducts that lurk in their toekicks can stay put too. Rather than make a room wider or longer, consider keeping the perimeter walls and vaulting the ceiling to the rafters: that cost (about $2,000 for this space) is about one quarter the cost of pushing an exterior wall out a couple of feet—and the feel is greatly expanding.

Keeping what's in place requires much tighter attention to detail and dimensions, as those parts that remain can bind unless the detailing allows for movement, storage, and very specific use patterns. Building new allows you to be lazy and just add a foot or too here and there. Recycling viable existing pieces and parts saves money but costs in design time to review how the new impacts the remaining.

A table becomes an island, while built-ins on the window wall and back wall make an opened-up space work.

The new windows are centered on the existing sink, and the upper cabinets carry the window detailing into the room.

Spaulted-maple and stainless steel are used to counterpoint the painted cabinets.

Setting standard cabinet boxes on feet that have solid oak "toes" allows the existing wood floor to continue under the island.

What not to do: a stove tight to the side cabinets, a window too small for anyone but the person at the sink to see outside.

BEFORE

Stone and steel are tough and lovely, glass provides contrast, and a valence brings light and scale down to the chef in a vaulted space.

BEFORE

New windows and cabinetry allow people and storage to feel at home.

The door, window, and floor are the same, but relocating the heat allows room for a seat and new cabinets create more storage.

Kitchen in a Condo

SELECTIVELY REMOVING a nonbearing wall (right) connects a viewless, internal kitchen to living and dining spaces. Simple, standard detailing was used to create custom cabinets at an affordable cost. Tall elements (range hood, refrigerator, and upper cabinets) were kept away from the opening to allow better connection; the height of the wall (3 ft. 8 in.) allows for a visual separation of whatever is on the countertop from those in the living room. Keeping the kitchen essentially where it was and simply opening it up saved money, and the chaos of construction was limited to a single area of the condo.

BEFORE

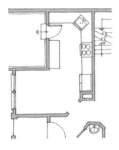

AFTER

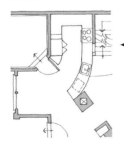

An interior kitchen is expanded and opened up to the living area. Relocating the connecting door to the garage allows for a full "C" of cabinetry.

Opening up a nonbearing wall without changing structure, pipes, or ducts makes visual connection and functional expansion possible.

The kitchen has become the hub of the house.

A lightly dropped beam, a raised lower cabinet wall, and a column hiding a pipe restrict views in to the kitchen while allowing full exposure out from the space.

BEFORE

go to **www. staying put.com** to see more of this project

Removing a wall, moving the refrigerator, and relocating the sink turned an inward kitchen inside out.

DUO'S DO'S & DON'TS

Curves cost: use where they work

Curves are frozen movement, drawing attention and delighting the eye—but they cost far more than the same piece of your house that is not curved. Walls that curve can cost perhaps four times more per linear foot than a straight-run version. A curved cabinet or trim milled to a curve can cost eight times more per running foot. Cutting countertops to a curve adds a degree of difficulty and creates waste that costs. Curved-top doors or windows can easily triple the cost of any unit. But sometimes, as in this kitchen, bending a wall to accommodate traffic flow or to catch a view can maximize efficiency and connect interior spaces.

PROJECT **Always Connect**

WHEN YOU SET OUT on the remodeling path, you sometimes have to deal with the very bad decisions of previous renovators. A 1960s renovation to an 1800s schoolhouse conversion created a dead-end kitchen that had a bizarre walk-around "baffle" separation between it and the dining room. Taking out half of the mini-maze wall and all of the central partition completely opened up the kitchen to the dining room. The creation of a deep wall of appliances and cabinetry and two peninsulas allowed for full integration with the large living space beyond. The deep wall hides the oven, TV, and refrigerator from the rest of the opened-up interior. All window locations stayed the same, which determined the placement of the peninsula cabinetry. A mini desk/phone station was set to one corner, and a legitimate breakfast bar allows visitors to sit and face the cooks.

BEFORE

AFTER

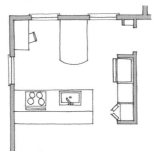

Removing the divider opened up the kitchen to the dining room.

With the divider removed, there's room for a large peninsula island for cooking, cleanup, and breakfast (foreground) and a smaller food-prep peninsula beyond.

The kitchen is the one room **that** needs to connect to every other public room in your house.

As well as a refrigerator, oven, and pantry, the deep wall also conceals a TV.

BEFORE

An opening in the deep wall provides access between the kitchen and dining room, where before there was none.

BEFORE

At the other end of the deep wall, the living room connects seamlessly with the dining room.

Sometimes You Have to Grow

ANTIQUE HOMES were never designed to have open kitchens, certainly not in the locations that today's homeowners want. Adding 6 ft. to the back of this 18th-century farmhouse allowed the galley kitchen to be relocated where it could become a full-blown U. The collateral benefit is that a new laundry/mudroom could be built where the existing kitchen was by relocating the laundry to the back door. In addition, a full mudroom was created, including pantry and broom closets, while maintaining the existing back door and window locations. Columns were incorporated into the kitchen's design to keep costs down, and a low wall keeps funky kitchen views separate from the living areas.

BEFORE

BEFORE   **AFTER**

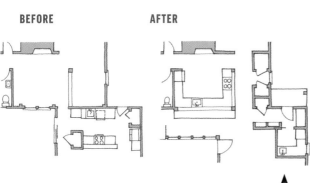

A 6-ft. addition creates space for the relocated kitchen—and a full mudroom and laundry in place of the old kitchen.

BEFORE

The new hallway allows people to get to anywhere else in the house without having to walk through the kitchen.

Showing structure is cheaper than hiding it

It is always less expensive to drop a beam below a floor than it is to set it up into the floor cavity. Laying floors on top of beams requires less thought, precision, and planning. It is always cheaper to have columns set under beams than to have a long open span. It always costs more to have one big beam above a window wall than to have structural supports between the windows breaking up the span. Whenever you try to make gravity disappear in the design of a building (this is often the great allure of modern homes), costs rise. If you can allow things like columns and beams to show themselves, you'll keep costs down.

A new mudroom occupies the
space of the original kitchen.

BEFORE

Change Is Good

BEFORE

A SMALL, late-19th-century in-town home had been turned it into a two-family rental at some point during the 1960s. The resulting first-floor kitchen was little more than a square interior room with standard appliances and a few out-of-the-box cabinets screwed to the walls. Hardly the place anyone would want to spend much time. When the home was reconstituted as a single-family residence, solving the storage problem was a top priority. This solution was found by taking out a nonbearing wall between the kitchen and the hallway and using the remaining long wall for shelving and cabinetry. The extra space created by removing the partition made room for an island and family-scale cooking while greatly improving the flow.

BEFORE

AFTER

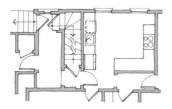
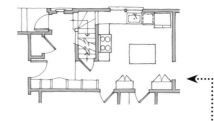

Taking out the nonbearing wall between the kitchen and the hallway was the key to opening up the kitchen.

Applying color, exposing brick, and using teak as a countertop material further enriched the newly opened up space.

BEFORE

By ganging together two windows that were once separate and opening up a portal to the back staircase, more light was allowed to flow through the space.

A long storage wall lines the hallway between the remodeled kitchen and an existing bedroom and bath.

DUO'S DO'S & DON'TS

Color is cheap

Drywall was made to be painted. The effect can be dramatic, especially when you mix and match the colors to provide contrast. Cool colors tend to recede and warm colors tend to be more present. When colors are coordinated, the modest cost of paint provides a bonanza of empowering impact. It is by far the least expensive way to completely transform any interior and can add snap to a shabby exterior—especially if contrast and complement are part of your color selection.

Combine and Expand

A 1970S RENOVATION to this 19th-century antique home cut a back door directly into a tacked-on bay, which made using the existing kitchen awkward at best—anyone entering the house had to walk through the kitchen to get anywhere in the rest of the house. This is an all-too-common problem. Removing a cramped full butler's pantry and sealing up several doors allowed a long L run of built-ins to be set to the two interior walls, creating continuous counter space and storage versus the broken-up and inefficient layout of the existing kitchen and pantry. By filling in a corner of the house to create a new rear door and mudroom, the aforementioned bay could be completely given over to banquette seating for family dining and the kitchen could accommodate a very large island and a small built-in desk all within an open plan.

The elaborate stove hood and cabinetry detailing grab attention in the newly flowing space.

BEFORE

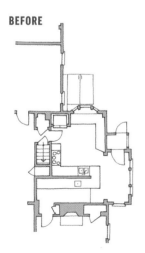

AFTER

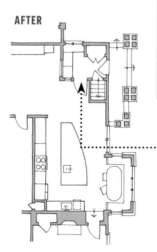

Adding a mudroom allows a whole new layout for the kitchen.

The back door previously opened directly into the eating bay.

BEFORE

Connection by Subtraction

IN THE ORIGINAL PLAN for this 1970s contemporary house, half the floor space was chopped up to create a kitchen, laundry, three-quarter bath, and back door. The removal of virtually all the nonbearing walls in that part of the plan allowed a tight U kitchen to expand into one that has a full island with pantry closets layered onto the remaining bearing wall. The powder room and laundry room were relocated to an existing rear shed popout that was previously unheated. Sink and stove locations were maintained to keep costs down, and new cabinetry respected the existing window locations, again saving money. The lack of structural and exterior work kept this major redo cost-effective. Demolition is cheap, and, if structurally viable, renovating unfinished unheated space is far less expensive than adding on.

BEFORE

BEFORE

AFTER

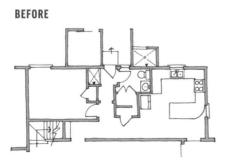

The existing peninsula island comes out, replaced by a long, sleek island with eat-in dining to one side.

BEFORE

The lack of structural and exterior work kept this major redo cost-effective.

A low wall separates the kitchen from the adjoining family room.

BEFORE

Demo is cheap

It stands to reason that something that takes a lot of thought takes more time to execute than mindless activity. Similarly, something that needs to be precise takes more preparation and control to execute. Time is money. Demolition is imprecise and takes precious little mindfulness—but it's not risk free. There are three things that can get you into trouble in demolition:

- You could knock something out that's holding something else up.

- You could smash through walls or floors and hit pipes or wires, gas, or waste lines that control very dangerous things (high pressure water, natural gas, electricity, and poop).

- Things that you are smashing and bashing into bits often contain chemicals, particulates, and gases that can kill you.

For this reason, it may make sense to hire a professional to do your demo work. Since demolition is not rocket science, it's pretty cheap. It costs about one tenth as much to remove a nonbearing wall as it does to build one (perhaps $50 to remove, $500 to put up). Conversely, when you have to relocate loads, things get a bit more pricey. But it certainly costs far less (perhaps $1,500) to remove part of a wall and to insert a big window than to add a sun room (perhaps $15,000).

When Curves Make Sense

THIS NEW KITCHEN in an apartment was painstaking shoe-horned into an exceptionally tight space (approximately 10 ft. by 15 ft.) that had only one wall that could give. And that wall had a steam pipe that needed to move with it—an expensive move because it impacted apartments above and below the space. By moving the wall (and pipe), a precisely sized island could be slipped into the widened space and allow cooking on one side while keeping wine sippers to the other. But even that dimensional relief required the use of curves to maximize storage capacity and maintain easy passage between the front entry to one side and family room to the other.

The use of the full existing 11-ft. ceiling allowed room for a "clerestory closet" of cabinetry that used more curves to create the extension of those upper level cabinets without a visual pinch. The presence of a large existing window next to the sink limited the standard location for upper cabinetry, which necessitated that pantry-style storage be part of the design (filling in a leftover corner that remained once the wall work was done).

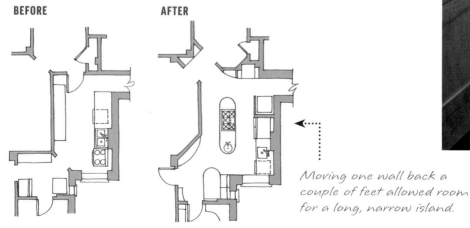

BEFORE

BEFORE   **AFTER**

Moving one wall back a couple of feet allowed room for a long, narrow island.

The curves continue in the cut of the upper cabinet above the sink.

Curves can help ease the limitations of tight spatial tolerances.

The kitchen is without question the king of cost-sucking activity in any renovation.

BEFORE

kitchen islands

It is now the norm to have a working kitchen island—a place that keeps visitors at a distance from the act of cooking but allows flow around it. The island is also a perfect place for artful expression because it forms visual distraction from the necessarily rude elements of technology needed to cook things (the bulky refrigerator box, whatever fan extracts odors from your cooktop, and the ever-present eye-level microwave and oven).

As the most-used and most visually present part of the kitchen, islands can cost as much as all the rest of the kitchen cabinets combined. As such they sometimes become wonderfully anomalous: a recycled piece of antique furniture, a custom-crafted piece of millwork (even if you use stock cabinetry it can support a $5,000 piece of stone or a $3,000 teak countertop). Islands are the focal point of carefully designed task lighting that allows for preparation, serving, and, yes, the display of those wonderful countertop materials to have maximum impact.

An existing window next to the sink imposed limits on the location of the upper cabinets.

Sliding in a banquet eating area in the tightest possible space provides a place to dine away from the cooking zone.

BEFORE

PROJECT Escaping the Dark Side

JACOBEAN STAINED-OAK cabinets may have been all the rage in 1970s suburban kitchens, but they look depressingly out of place today. Working within the existing footprint and keeping the window and sink locations, this dark kitchen was completely transformed with focused lighting and natural-finish white oak cabinets that feel like furniture.

A careful relocation of the refrigerator opened up counter space along the outside wall, but required a new island orientation that responded to the narrowing of the kitchen space (there's still room for a quick bite at the island's public side). The cooktop was relocated away from the dining room to the outside wall, keeping cooking away from dining and enhancing both spaces. Though new cabinets, countertops, and appliances were a considerable expense, money was saved by keeping wall removal to a minimum (at an unused area of the adjacent bath), doing no structural work, and maintaining the existing flooring and door and window locations.

BEFORE

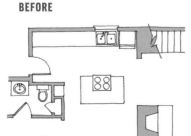

AFTER

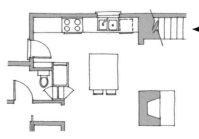

The footprint's the same, but it's all change for the appliances and cabinetry.

Cabinets define the look of the kitchen more than any other item.

kitchens and code

Beyond all the mechanical and functional demands, the kitchen is subjected to more code restrictions than any other room in the house. The quantity and availability of outlets is precisely determined. The wall behind your cooktop has to be heat shielded (not unlike the surround of your fireplace). If your oven is self-cleaning, it generates enough heat that there has to be an appropriate separation between it and anything that is combustible and venting space is often required. High-output stoves have venting requirements for their BTUs and COs. Commercial stove/oven combinations used in houses also have fire separation requirements to cabinetry.

BEFORE

In keeping with the kitchen remodel, a fireplace was resurfaced in the adjoining living room.

*Plenty was altered in
this kitchen remodel, but
the door and window
locations and the flooring
remained unchanged.*

BEFORE

Doing the Open Up!

AS IS TYPICAL of most Raised Ranches, the original kitchen was enclosed by walls on all four sides. Taking out the walls between the kitchen and dining room and kitchen and living room completely opened the space for public consumption.

Two columns replaced the load-bearing wall between the kitchen and the living room; the relocated weight had to be carried through to the basement below to bear on the ground. While most walls were removed, adding a new short wall at the edge of the kitchen shields off the side view of the refrigerator from the front door beyond.

Costs were contained by keeping an existing skylight and the window and sink location, while relocating a door to the outside created room for a pantry. Not only was the kitchen space enlarged by removing the walls but it was also made more versatile with the addition of an island.

BEFORE

BEFORE   **AFTER**

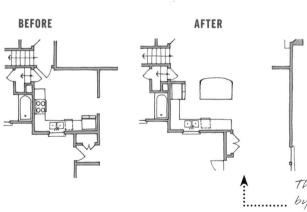

The walls are gone (replaced by two columns), an island is added, and the skylight remains.

Removing the walls directly connects the kitchen, living, and dining rooms into one flowing ensemble of spaces.

Lose a Bathroom, Grow the Kitchen

IN A TURN-OF-THE-20TH-CENTURY suburban house, a very tight kitchen and bath were combined to create a two-part kitchen—half for cooking, half for pantry and pastry. Changing the location of the rear door allowed for a full U configuration (replacing the old galley layout), and using custom cabinetry takes advantage of every cubic inch of space. A desk, bar, and pastry-kneading countertop (3 in. lower than all the others) was built into a very small, low, and previously stepped space (floor levels were brought up to the higher main level, which is much cheaper than lowering one level to meet the other). The floor finish is a one-off art piece involving painting and a high-tech curing process. All existing structure was maintained, but celebrated by the removal of layers of "decorative arts" (wallpaper and paint) and the application of a simple whitewash.

▶ go to **www. staying put.com** to learn why too many outlets and lights are better than too few

BEFORE

AFTER

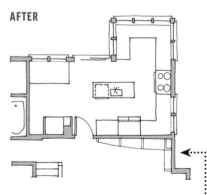

Taking over the bathroom creates enough room for a fully functioning kitchen.

BEFORE

Glass block used
as a backsplash
for the stove brings
in more light and
facilitates cleaning.

Kitchen in a Box

THERE ARE TIMES when you can't afford to change the footprint of a kitchen, and then there are times when it's physically impossible to break out of the existing box. A concrete barn built at the turn of the century was converted to a home in the 1950s, and all of its walls and window openings were literally cast in place. The owners wanted to create a great deal more storage capacity than the original kitchen had, and the only option was to use custom cabinetry that allowed every cubic inch to be accessed. This was done by careful use of hardware and fitting the cabinetry precisely to the fixed doors and windows. But adding more storage can mean a greater sense of constriction in a small space that cannot have more or larger openings to the outside world. So this design uses open shelving above the cooking area and a flush solid-surface backsplash material that visually opens up the space.

Although the cabinetry—with its stainless-steel appointments, beautiful maple interiors, extraordinary hardware, and custom design—was quite costly, the rest of the costs of this project were minimized by the fact that no walls or openings could be changed in any way. What results is a completely new kitchen in a completely unchanged room that has larger storage capacity and less visual confinement.

Open shelving visually opens up the tight space.

The cherry cabinets are inspired by Shaker millwork and furniture, and their level of detail and craft follows through on the focus that a small space affords.

PROJECT **Creating a Cook's Kitchen**

A UNIQUE KITCHEN design for a serious cook was imposed on a small 1910 house that was split into two units in the 1920s. The remodel recombined the units into a single-family home, and four spaces were given over for the new kitchen: the original dining room, the family room, a bath, and the tiny kitchen. The new, open-layout kitchen centers around a "cooking wall," and also comprises a large island, a cleanup wall, and a pantry (behind the cooking wall). Effectively two pantries—one for "show" opposite the dining area and one for storage (next to the exterior cleanup sink)—make this a fully optioned kitchen in a tight space. The existing full bathroom bit the dust and was reduced to a powder room built where a relocated staircase used to be.

BEFORE

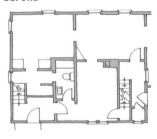

AFTER

Looking through from the dining room.

The kitchen is divided by function into three spaces: cooking place (the island and cooktop); cleanup space (at the window wall); and pantry and ovens (behind the cooktop wall).

Extreme versatility, storage capacity, and visual delight combine in a carefully crafted design.

BEFORE

the pantry

The vast majority of kitchens, even small ones, demand pantry space that is at least as big as a bedroom closet but preferably as big as a small master suite walk-in closet. The overwhelming desire is to minimize the number of upper cabinets that are visually present in most kitchens (limited to those around dishwashers where they are needed to store everyday dinnerware and glassware). Upper cabinets close in the space at eye level, preventing windows and visual connection beyond the kitchen.

4

Living rooms & social spaces

Multiple spaces can multitask if there is careful planning and enough light and space to keep things open.

The classic American living room has gone the way of the plastic slip cover.

Perhaps even less part of our current culture than the formal dining room, the touch-me-not living room has been dramatically changed by the great transition of the American family from stay-at-home moms and one-income families to accommodating work coming home 24/7.

Formal dinner parties where people have cocktails in the living room, adjourn to the dining room, and then back to the living room for coffee is a social dance that has pretty much ceased to exist.

House design, like the design of all buildings, follows the way buildings are used. The new paradigm is that the entire family needs to decompress at home, and cooking has become fun for everyone. People need a place to connect without having a kitchen countertop as an intermediary, so social space now extends from the kitchen.

You can get more out of your house without having to create more house.

When these social changes began to transform how we used our social spaces, our houses adapted in a very familiar pattern: by adding space. Dramatic informal spaces launched themselves off of the kitchen hub, ending up in the great room of the 1970s and 1980s. Those inflated spaces typically just added more space to homes that already had seldom-used living and dining rooms.

With the rising cost of energy and everything else, duplicating square footage and bulking up on cubic footage while the number of people occupying the home remained constant was insane. So the paradigm has shifted again. For the most part, the projects shown in this chapter are internal remodeling: When new space is added, it is at a carefully calculated minimum and thoughtfully interwoven with the existing interior. In new home designs and in rethinking existing homes, the segregation of social spaces from the kitchen and both of those functions from

before & AFTER

Killing a corner by widening an existing opening greatly increases the sense of space.

outdoor living is coming to an end. Of course, traditional isolated room layouts are perfect for some families, but these are becoming fewer and fewer.

Downsizing the great room

It's a cliché to say that people are doing more with less, but these projects show that you can get more out of your house without having to create more house. Typically, this means removing walls and increasing the connection with the outdoors both visually and functionally. This approach requires thinking about your present home not as a confining box but as a place that you can take control of.

ABOVE: Built-ins were a priority in this second-floor informal social space in a remodeled Bungalow, which combines workout room, TV viewing, and library.

FACING PAGE: Where once was a narrow doorway, a widened, arched-top opening now provides a better connection to the dining room beyond.

The growing trend supplanting the knee-jerk blow-out of an outsize great room is to actually have a comfortable place to sit virtually in the kitchen—not on awkward stools at the island but on a soft, comfy sofa that can accommodate any number of physical postures. It's the kind of space that will accommodate good lighting, soft sitting places, casual eating, and reading material. Space for these pieces of furniture and activities might take up a 12-ft. by 18-ft. area in addition to the kitchen.

Eating is obviously part of the informal social experience and has a critical impact on the way you renovate your home. Think about the true number of people that will eat informally in or near the kitchen. That's usually the size of your family plus two people at maximum. Obviously, diners could sit at a kitchen island or the extension of a counter or a peninsula of cabinets, but more than ever people want to connect to the outside so a glass

where are they now? the great room

The mindless gigantism of the great room has left the building. Gone from new construction, the great room's literal echoes resonate amid the lost heat of its inflated air bag of space and its unwashable double-height glass walls. The loss of the great room from new homes being built in today's market tends to reduce the overall size of the average house. Its absurd blankness has caused reconsideration of how we actually use the living spaces in our house.

The great room was designed for one thing: shock appeal for potential buyers awed at the idea of such a huge space being part of a house. This wow factor turned into an oh-no factor when the utility bills started arriving, the TV was turned on, or teenagers gathered. After perhaps 5 years of occupancy, the window walls' exterior trim began to rot and windows started to become inoperable. Inevitably, a massive investment had to be made in blinds, curtains, and other sun-control devices as the view out also let the sun in.

But the great room was a radical response to an earlier dysfunction. The vast majority of traditional house plans built in America before the 1970s had little or no informal living space. Basements were finished, a TV was put in a guest bedroom, or a sun room was tacked on the home to allow the family to share time together. Pre-1970s designs assumed Mom and Dad sat in the living room with a cocktail and a cigarette, while the children busied themselves in their rooms.

So the trick is to create informal living space in a home but avoid the wasteful overkill of the great room. This means renovating your home to reflect the way you live.

bay or a corner of windows is becoming part of the informal dining area design.

With carefully considered budgets, the owners of these projects spent strategically to remove barriers, open vistas, and make the kind of spatial connections that are dictated by the way we use our homes today. The net result is an informal integrated flow of interior space that is allowed to connect transparently to the great outdoors.

MOST AMERICAN suburban homes have more walls than people want. There are two types of walls in most homes: those that carry weight (bearing walls) and those that don't (nonbearing walls). Removing walls that carry weight means that you have to have beams and columns to carry that load down through the home to the ground. Walls that act only as curtains can simply be pulled back and removed.

In this typical small suburban Cape, there were a few walls too many, so those were removed to fully connect the living spaces. In the living room where an existing column had to be pulled back to accommodate a new entry path, the end of the existing beam was left to cantilever to carry the load above but its underside was cut to a gentle curve to make a potentially awkward element a visual feature. Similarly, a staircase that divided the two social areas of the house had been enclosed by two walls and those two areas were further separated by a door. By leaving the stairs in place, removing all the walls above the stringers (the diagonal trim on either side of the steps themselves) and the door, and adding an open railing, maximum visual connection was achieved.

▶ go to **www.staying put.com** to see more of this project

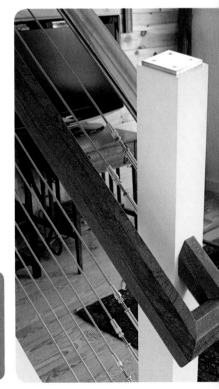

The walls on either side of the stairs were removed, providing better visual connection between the front half of the house and the back.

BEFORE

BEFORE

Light curves and tapers in the column shroud and beam trim make the needed support an artful addition.

A section of floor was removed to get added openness and top-lighting from a new window array at the peak of the new vaulted space.

BEFORE

can I take that wall out?

Most homes in America fall into a few distinct types—Cape, Ranch, Foursquare, center hall Colonial—and each has some predictable structural approaches. Basements usually tell the truth that's otherwise hidden by ceiling and wall surfaces. The Cape typically has one bearing wall that parallels its street-facing front wall, but many Capes built before the 20th century are post-and-beam structures, and so in truth the chimney bears the center loads and there are posts in the perimeter walls.

Similarly, the Ranch can have a center bearing condition that parallels the front wall but often transitions to be 90 degrees to it at the open, social end. The Foursquare can have bearing walls in any direction of its pinwheel layout. In about 95 percent of old Colonials the hall walls are the bearing walls, but newer homes can have a center bearing wall paralleling the front. Any home that is asymmetrical (Contemporary, Victorian, Mediterranean) can be framed in any way imaginable, but normally the shorter room dimension is the direction of the floor framing.

The unpredictability of framing is usuall the first hurdle you have to get over when you want to remodel your home in terms of cost prediction. There is no way builders or architects can know precisely which way the framing runs if all the floors and walls are sealed up, unless they break through finish surfaces before they start figuring out structural design (and thus determine cost). It's possible to make reasonable assumptions, but, as the Boy Scouts say, "Be Prepared."

Open-Minded

IN A 1920S hillside upside-down house, where the living area is below the entry level, walking downstairs to get to the living room wasn't the only aspect that was awkward. When you arrived at the living floor you were unceremoniously dumped into a tight vestibule measuring just 6 ft. by 4 ft. with three 3-ft. doorways providing access into each space. By removing one nonbearing wall between the stairs and the dining room and kitchen and by opening the bearing wall between the dining room and the living area, all three spaces were able to flow.

It would have been easy enough just to remove walls and let the space speak for itself, but instead a carefully crafted frame was used to make the opening to the living room from the rest of the floor an event. The playful trim-out also announces a level change (two steps down) that gives the living space a sense of heightened stature. By integrating a new fireplace front with the new trim and carefully harvesting tiles from other places in the remodeled house, continuity was achieved without blowing the budget.

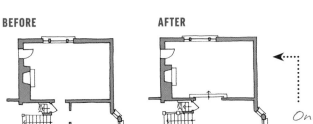

BEFORE   **AFTER**

One nonbearing wall comes out, and the opening in the bearing wall is widened.

Stripping away the tangle of walls and doorways at the bottom of the entry stairs allows the living area to flow.

BEFORE

Most American suburban homes have more walls than people want.

The width of the new opening between the dining room and the living room was limited on one side by a waste line that would have been too costly to move (the opening is still over 6 ft. wide even with the pipe remaining in place).

BEFORE

DUO'S DO'S & DON'TS

If you walk through a room to get to a room, something is wrong

Many times additions layer onto homes, so you have to walk through the archaeological history of your home to get to a new space. Investigate the cost of simply removing walls and doing a smaller addition rather than a larger addition that bypasses an existing space. That bypassed space is bigger than a hallway but functions as one and betrays the capacity of your home to be renewed with enhanced efficiency.

BEFORE

The trim around the
opening is carefully
integrated with the
new fireplace trim.

PROJECT Always Connect

A SIMPLE EXTENSION of living space in place of an existing deck combines a new informal family room with an existing dining space to expand a classic Raised Ranch. Beyond the actual increase in floor area by 14 ft. by 20 ft., the impact of the added space was greatly enhanced by two simple moves. First, taking out the wall between the new space and the house as well as expanding an existing opening to the living area unify old and new. Second, by vaulting the new living space ceiling and removing the dining room ceiling to create a complementary vault, the home's interior flows up as well as out. The new ceiling trim treatment of ribs and tongue-and-groove paneling further unifies a flowing sense of openness that is achieved between old and new.

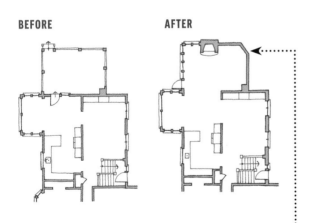

BEFORE   **AFTER**

The corner of the family room had to be clipped back to conform to the local zoning setback.

Top-lighting the new room with clerestory windows allows daylight to flow all the way back to the existing kitchen.

BEFORE

The new family room sits on the footprint of the old deck.

Expanding without Adding On

BEFORE

SOMETIMES THE WAY the existing space in your home is laid out makes it difficult to use or appreciate its overall dimensions. In a 1980s addition to a classic early-19th-century Federal, a layer of living space was simply wrapped around the perimeter of the existing home's backside, with doorways cut through the original outside walls. The kitchen was thus visually cut off from the informal living space, and the resulting wrap-around room was rarely used. Removing those walls was conceptually easy, but the second floor above the wall had to be supported. Fortunately, the old one-story addition presented the opportunity to hide the beam that replaced the original exterior wall above the ceiling level. By setting the new beam in the cavity above the ceiling but below the old addition's roofline, the original ceiling does not get interrupted by a dropped beam.

In this project, two custom birch columns supplanted a long bearing wall, and a large amount of millwork that was layered on the old outside walls of the home was replaced by an island cabinet between the columns. In addition, the raw 1980s ceiling was furred down to create a peak within the formerly sawtoothed ceiling-scape.

BEFORE

AFTER

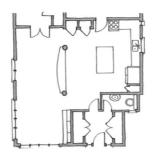

One side of the new island provides storage and a place for the TV, while the back side accommodates space for informal dining.

BEFORE

The wall of cabinets was replaced by two columns and an island cabinet.

A GREENHOUSE was tacked onto this classic 1960s Contemporary home in the 1970s. In the current remodel, the add-on was removed and a new glass-filled end for the living space was built on the existing foundation. Taking out the sliding-glass doors that separated the living room from the greenhouse and opening up the space to the new gable roof meant that the signature large-scale structure of 2× framing and steel flitch plate reinforcement could be exposed. The resulting space is spiritually in sync with the original architect "statement" home but now actually sheds water, provides greater insulation, and makes an open vista from the low end of a descending roofline.

BEFORE

Opening up the interior also entailed replacing the narrow, steep, and ugly existing stairs with a gentle, open staircase made of teak.

BEFORE

With the remodel, a slot was cut through the existing roof to create a ridge skylight that unifies the living room and the new sun room.

▶ go to www.
**staying
put.com**
for more about
Contemporary
homes

Getting the '80s Out

BEFORE

WE ALL KNOW that paint is one of the easiest ways to transform a space, but trim can also work design wonders. Here, new linear trim was carefully applied to extend and connect the lines that were already there—the edge of a balcony, window mullions (the spaces between the windows and doors), and the existing chimney mass and fireplace. The trim was built on site from flat stock and clear-finished cherry. As important as the added trim was removing elements such as the low walls that supported catalog-cliché columns, which transformed the visual flow and eliminated the artificial division between dining and living spaces. A tacked-on stock crown molding was stripped from the fireplace front in favor of the simple lines of solid cherry and subtle millwork detailing. Color was also used to reinforce the fireplace's identity, and strategic lighting was applied to enhance the lines the new trim created.

BEFORE

Taking out the low walls with columns opened up the floor plan.

A Contemporary home with Postmodern stylistic affectations was cleaned up with trim, color, and a fair amount of demo of the fussy builder detailing that was so prevalent 20 years ago.

BEFORE

In the dining area, the trim lines were extended to create a shelf that wraps around a corner above windows and doors.

Built-ins take advantage of the new bay-window bump-out.

Taking Over a Sun Room

BEFORE

IT IS ALWAYS CHEAPER to build on an existing foundation, as long as it can handle the weight of the new construction. When this house was built in the 1920s, cars were not part of the master planning of most suburban homes. In a community of tight suburban lots, a garage-less stucco Tudor had one added after World War II that was simply a flat-roofed terrace with space for two cars below it. In the 1960s, the classic jalousied windowed sun room was added, set on the perimeter wall of that garage-top terrace to create a three-season room (which is actually a two-season room—too hot in the summer and too cold in the winter to actually use).

The current owners, who have young children, knew that they needed more living space than the small house could provide and saw their unused sun room as staked-out territory for vertical expansion. The existing garage was built within the zoning setbacks, and through some careful manipulation of the roof shape, existing windows could either be brought into the double-height interior space or allowed to remain on the exterior wall. The new window design on the broad gable end of the addition overtly follows through on the Tudor half-timbering of the original home and even the detailing of the mahogany millwork picks up on the lines of that stylistic generator.

The current remodel expands on a sun room that was added atop the garage in the 1960s.

A strategic skylight enhances a sense of openness, while custom millwork takes advantage of the verticality of the new space.

Building on an existing foundation is always cheaper than building on a new foundation.

5

Connecting to the outdoors

Walls can be opened to connect to the outdoors, but care must be taken or you simply chop holes in your house.

In my experience, the greatest trend in residential architecture over the last 10 to 20 years has been the desire of homeowners to connect their homes to the environment.

This desire to be outside and protected has been infused into almost every space I deal with as an architect. This newfound naturalist imperative may well have taken hold in compensation for the increasing amount of time everyone spends in front of the video screens that we use for work and entertainment on an almost round-the-clock basis. The screaming need for relief from the glowing face of our social networks, work products, spreadsheets, games, DVDs, and photographs makes the need for offline elements of our home palpable and growing.

Virtual reality ain't reality and we know it. But we want a nonvirtual reality tempered with protection and comfort. The ultimate physical reality outside of ourselves is the great outdoors—and our homes can connect us to it as well as protect us from its hazards. There is a menu of options, each with a different price tag, that you should be aware of before you jump into remodeling a home that was probably originally designed as a Skinner box of domestic drudgery.

Opening up to the outside

The vast majority of all dwellings in America were intended to be dropped onto any site and thus no one particular place. These homes were typically designed in traditional styles of architecture by which windows were isolated and regularly placed. Their interiors were laid out with no particular residents in mind, and, worse, they were completely ignorant of everything outside their walls.

One of the best ways to make these dead boxes come alive and be yours is to put them on a 12-step program for recovery. Most homes need a fair amount of hug therapy when it comes to giving them the confidence to reach out into the great wild-and-wooly world. Most of our homes built before 1970 were viewed as latter-day caves, places of safety rather than comfort. Homes have always been places where people retreat from the harsh working environment to the soft environment of family comfort. Escaping to the television set is no longer the central focus of what many people want in their nonwork lives because they look at a virtual television set—either held in their hand, sitting on the desk in front of them, or sitting on their lap—most of the day. The pressure to look away from an artificial glow to a sunlit open world is becoming unavoidable—and houses are responding. Since it seems

that few of us are going to retire anymore, we can at least retire when we go home to an alternative reality, the real world. As we'll see in the rest of this chapter, there are several ways of connecting to the outdoors.

Looking out

Seeing out is not as good as being out, but at least it means that you are not standing in the rain. De-boxing your house via windows is a very effective way to make the focus go beyond your walls. However, installing windows and doors is not without cost. Any time you cut out whole parts from the body of your house, it costs, so don't perform unnecessary elective surgery. Each new opening costs at least $500, and that can easily double or triple for

**before &
AFTER**

The typical traditional layout of the openings of a center hall Colonial provides little opportunity to get the broad sweep of exterior connection to the outdoors that most people now want. Obviously, you can always throw in large-scale glass doors, picture windows, or bay windows, but these are limited to a one-sided view. Here, a three-sided addition to a 1980s Colonial home effectively overcomes the rest of the house's ignorance of the beautiful woods and gardens that surround it.

ABOVE: We don't often think of a basement as a space that can have views outside, but there are exceptions. In this addition to a waterside home, the basement was originally designed to be fully buried without a view. But the view wall was on the side of the house where the ground fell away, and a simple relocation of the earth provides a sight line to water.

each new window or door. Spend to get views and access, not on general principle. Don't forget that glass can allow the sun to bake you in summer and the winter chill to empty your wallet in the winter.

Walking out

It is one thing to look through glass, but it is another to actually get outside. Many traditional homes (Capes and Colonials) have one front door and one back door and force you to walk through rooms to exit. If anything, the impetus for many people is to have multiple points of access to the outdoors.

New openings obviously mean more maintenance and allow more air in and out of a home. Quality doors cost two or three times as much as mediocre ones ($1,200 vs. $400) but will pay for themselves in a decade because they usually keep a better seal and need less maintenance in the out years. Sliding doors are always less expensive than swinging doors and don't impose their swings inside or outside your home, but they do tend to be harder to operate over time and also tend to leak more air.

windows have multiple personalities

Windows have three unique functions. First, they let you look out and see things. Second, they let light into your house so that you can see things when you're inside (if the sun is out). Third, they bring outside air into your house so that you feel comfortable inside. There is also a fourth function your windows share with the rest of your house: sealing against weather, either protecting against the unwanted invasion of water into your home (in the form of rain) or against air that is different in temperature from what you desire inside your home.

Most of our homes built before 1970 were viewed as latter-day caves, places of safety rather than comfort.

Creating an outdoor room for dining and relaxation can be as simple as adding a trellis over an existing terrace. This crafty construction of stained, pressure-treated wood is much less expensive than a roofed room addition.

Doors should be located in places that make it easy to get to whatever grade is present outside. Typically, spec homes are built slightly higher than they should be because it is cheaper and easier to dig a shallower hole and loft the building up. This means that many ground floors are 2 ft. to 4 ft. higher than their surrounding grade. Bringing in more dirt (setting it carefully to avoid your wood structure and not cause rot) allows you to make a quick-and-easy transition out to a terrace. This instant relief from entrapment for a dining room, a living room, or even a kitchen transforms traditional box homes.

Being out

The next logical step to walking out is to have a place to walk out to. Decks are more expensive than simple patios built on sand over dirt and need more maintenance, but they can create a transformative outdoor space.

Decks are often the only way to easily transition from a first-floor living space down to the lower walkout level of your basement. But decks also have exquisitely ugly undersides, and it's a big mistake to put them in full view of a walkout basement. A fair amount of water also gets under the deck as gapped decking is far more affordable than a deck that tries to shed water. If you are thinking about creating a room under your deck, think again. Although it is possible, it can be incredibly expensive, requiring a membrane roof under the decking.

Ladder-like, straight-run stairs that get you down to grade (as seen in so many rickety, spindly columned decks) are ugly and less safe than the softly transitional

BELOW: A low-lying deck off this remodeled home provides a spot for outdoor activity close to both cooking and living spaces.

A 1980s Contemporary had a screened porch big enough for eating or sitting (but not both) and a deck set one story above grade with no way to get down. By extending the existing detailing, porch and deck now reach out to a terrific view and backyard.

approach. Dropping a deck 3 ft. or 4 ft. down from the house floor is an effective way to keep the view from the inside and yet make the transition down to your backyard easier. Deck steps can be easily made into stadium seating to allow large groups of people to sit.

The way decking and the railings that surround them are detailed is key to how a deck is perceived. Open-step risers are both ugly and somewhat dangerous. Miters in decking edges that transition around corners always open up. Raw, unsanded end grain that is left exposed doesn't wear well. Decks need to be treated more like the finished trim in your house than the raw framing beneath the drywall and siding of your house. Unfortunately, the vast majority of decks follow the latter ethic.

Porches

Front porches in new homes have become romantic elements that developers use to sell shoddy houses in too-tight neighborhoods. Most of them never get used because they are just too narrow and face the street that has people on it who you never want to see. However, back porches that have views can be blissful if they are large enough. Just like decks, material choice and detailing are exquisitely important but unlike the deck, there is a whole other level of potential visual and functional disaster—the roof and its support.

Using double-helix twisted pressure-treated 4 × 4 posts with through knots, jagged edges, and gaping cracks can create a real eyesore when you look out to the view. It is always a good idea to put a layer of finished material around such rot-resistant supports and plastic trim works at a reasonable price.

When you are inside your house and looking through any opening into your porch, the underside of the porch roof is unavoidably present. A grooved-plywood ceiling is less expensive than painted solid wood; clear, natural wood may be lovely but can be a bit overpowering; stucco can be surprisingly affordable. A simple ceiling treatment

BELOW: A renovated informal living space (right) pinwheels with a screened porch (center left) and the kitchen (far left), creating a classic triad of informal living, cooking, and eating, all focused on exterior views.

Most front porches never get used because they are just too narrow.

of a neutral color may actually end up reinforcing what you want to do best—focus on the outdoors.

But it is the height of the ceiling that actually makes the most difference as experienced from inside and outside. If you maintain the height of your existing interior roof (typically 8 ft.), perspective causes the view to get pinched as you look out. A porch ceiling height of 9 ft., 10 ft., or even 12 ft. can transform a confining space into a protected outdoor experience. Porch roofs are visually important from the outside as well. How they interact with both your roofscape in a one-story house and the windows of the second story in a multistory house is critical.

If you are considering a large porch that is both wide and deep, be aware that it will cut light off to the interior of your home. You can add skylights to mitigate this, but the effect is never the same. If you locate the porch to allow an unfettered view from the rest of your house to the outdoors and provide very quick and easy access to the porch (typically from informal living space and/or the kitchen), it will actually get used.

THREE-SEASON ROOMS Many people fantasize about incorporating a three-season room into their home, which typically has single-paned glass in an unheated, unconditioned space that can be opened to get the full effect of a screened porch. While a three-season room does potentially

BELOW: A screened porch keeps animals and insects out and allows you to have a full and wonderful exposure to the outside world. It is more expensive than a regular porch because it involves screen doors and the frames for the screens, but ultimately it creates a greater sense of an outdoor room versus simply an outdoor space.

work, to me it is a "tweener" with all the disadvantages of an unheated, unconditioned space and a fair amount of its costs. It also requires a fair bit of monitoring to open and close the windows at the swing seasons depending on how warm, cold, or inclement it is.

SUN ROOMS A glass box that extends the treated air of your house (heated and cooled), a sun room has the full cost of any addition or perhaps more because windows are more expensive per square foot than an opaque framed wall. The space will be a gigantic heat sink in the winter and potentially a heat magnet in the summer. Deep eaves (overhangs) of more than 2 ft. are a necessity to prevent window wear and tear, overheating, and rainwater intrusion. In fact, the sun room is the most expensive addition you can do that doesn't involve plumbing. Its need for huge volumes of treated air necessitates a separate zone to maintain comfort when temperatures are only slightly out of the comfort zone.

Antique homes have real issues when it comes to connecting to the outside world. Often designed to retain the tiny amount of heat that their fireplaces would provide, they typically come factory equipped with tiny windows, very few doors, and (in colder climates anyway) limited porches. In this project, an early-19th-century in-town Colonial home gains a generous screened porch, which replaced a blank west-facing terrace set off an early ell-wing addition. The trim and detailing of the columns, mullions, and eaves are at a level that lives up to the care and craft of the original home's interiors (and were designed well enough to gain Historic District board approval).

Basic Moves Well Made

SOMETIMES IT DOESN'T TAKE MUCH to make better outdoor connections to a house. Here an existing brick patio was accessed by a single sliding door. That door was kept, but the rotting wood deck that brought people over to the brick patio was replaced by a set of bluestone steps; a new set of steps was added to the opposite side of the terrace, allowing double access by adding doors.

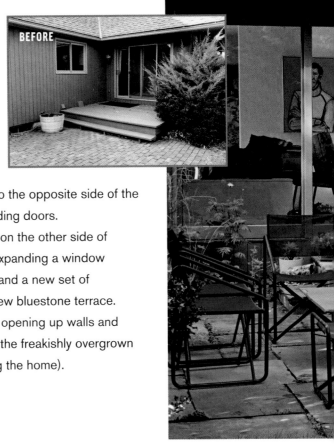

BEFORE

A second terrace was also added on the other side of the home, and this was facilitated by expanding a window opening to create a large sliding door and a new set of simple wraparound steps to another new bluestone terrace. Sometimes getting out is as simple as opening up walls and inserting new doors (and cutting back the freakishly overgrown foundation plants that were consuming the home).

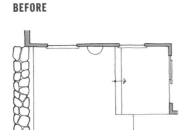

BEFORE

AFTER

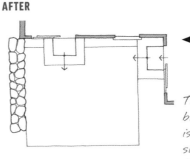

The new bluestone terrace is accessed by sliding doors from two sides.

BEFORE

Replacing the existing brick with salvaged flagstones allowed for an amazing visual transformation.

Another terrace was added on the other side of the house.

Wraparound Paradise

AN 18TH-CENTURY Federal farmhouse had multiple lean-to additions tacked onto it over its first 200 years. These served not so much to reach out to the landscape but to separate those within the house from it. In addition, plantings that were once under control began to consume not only the home's walls but also any potential for a view from the windows that actually caught a glimpse of a backyard pond.

The new owners removed all of the overgrown foliage and built a carefully crafted deck that celebrated its supports (rather than having apologetic pipes or spindly 4 × 4 pressure-treated posts).

Stainless-steel cable rails provide a code-compliant barrier without blocking the view, and mahogany rails afford a nice location to rest an afternoon cocktail. By using the existing stone steps that accessed the back door of the house and extending that line to create a simple L deck, the original flow of the house is maintained and a reasonable area for a table is created without visually separating the inside from the outside.

BEFORE

▶ go to www.stayingput.com

for more on the perils of foundation plantings

Using stainless-steel cables rather than wood balusters allows a clear view from the deck . . . and complies to code.

When a Deck Isn't Enough

THE ORIGINAL CONNECTION to the outdoors for this basic Cape/ Foursquare was a 1970s deck tacked onto its south side. It was a place that not only baked its occupants but also

BEFORE

subjected them to unending bug bites, and its eroding pressure-treated wood ugliness was an eyesore that was tough to ignore from inside the house. A straightforward add-on of a screened porch to the deck's perimeter was called for (and got through zoning because of the preexisting deck's violation of the setback), though the end result is anything but straightforward.

By condensing the new screened porch's structure to a few large-scale isolated elements (two huge microlam beams sitting on two columns plus as few screen-dividing mullions as possible), wide areas of screen make a very open inside–outside connection. By carefully keeping the screened porch's roofscape to a low pitch, existing windows on the second floor of the house were maintained. Two doors to the yard ensure traffic flow around the existing atrium doors of the home.

A screened porch offers the best of all worlds: It keeps animals and insects out and allows you to have a full and wonderful exposure to the outside world.

A monitor roof centered over the porch provides daylighting from above.

A cast-concrete floor stays cool under cover and was cheaper than building a raised wood-framed floor.

A New Old Porch

BEFORE

TACKED ON TO an early-19th-century center hall Colonial, the century-old porch was on the verge of collapse when the homeowners bought the house. Its decaying condition was out of sight and mind because the porch had no visual or functional connection to the home's interior. By eliminating the wall that separated the interior of the home from the porch and by completely rebuilding within the porch's original perimeter, the homeowners brought the outside in. Keeping the same shape and carefully detailing the casement windows to complement the existing double-hungs of the house meant it was an easy fit with the Historic District of the New England village. Money was saved by reusing the existing foundation.

The porch's casement windows are carefully detailed to complement the existing double-hungs on the main house.

Taking out the wall between the house
and the porch gets ample light into the
kitchen, which was also remodeled.

Terrace a-Go-Go

A CONCRETE TERRACE that was tacked onto a house in the 1960s was high enough that it had code-mandated railings all around its perimeter. But its height and railings meant that the view of a nearby pond from the family room wing was completely obscured. The rebuilt flagstone terrace kept the existing footings and foundation, but it was lowered by 18 in.; steps replaced the railings at the view side. By building in a barbeque to one side, the mobile chaos of rolling cooking equipment was eliminated and site lines from inside the house were further enhanced. The net result hardly touched the existing house but completely transformed the way the house was used in the summer months.

BEFORE

BEFORE

A built-in barbecue streamlines outdoor cooking on the terrace.

Lowering the height of the terrace and replacing the railing with steps opened up the view to a pond.

Inside Out

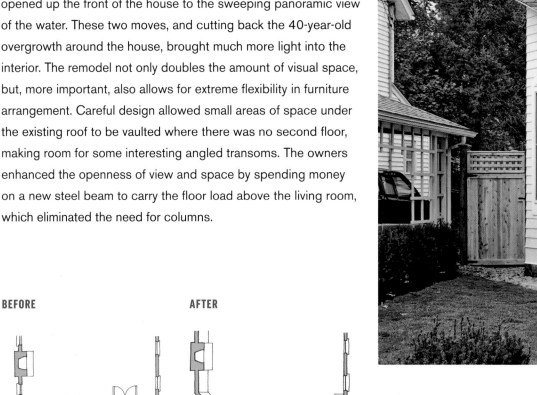

BEFORE

ADDING ON TO get a view is not always the best option; sometimes it's better to take something away. In this particular case, clipping back the solid corners of the existing porch and removing the inner wall that separated the porch from the living room opened up the front of the house to the sweeping panoramic view of the water. These two moves, and cutting back the 40-year-old overgrowth around the house, brought much more light into the interior. The remodel not only doubles the amount of visual space, but, more important, also allows for extreme flexibility in furniture arrangement. Careful design allowed small areas of space under the existing roof to be vaulted where there was no second floor, making room for some interesting angled transoms. The owners enhanced the openness of view and space by spending money on a new steel beam to carry the floor load above the living room, which eliminated the need for columns.

BEFORE   **AFTER**

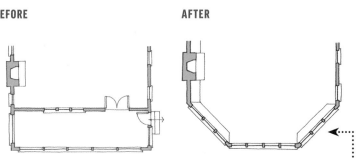

Adding on to get a view is not always the best option; sometimes it's better to take something away.

Less is more: Clipping back the corners of the porch and taking away the foundation plantings opened the house to a 180-degree view.

The remodel took out the existing wall between the porch and the living room.

BEFORE

Big views should have big openings

Picture yourself looking in a mirror. If the mirror is small, you have to get very close to it to see your face. If the mirror is hung too low, you have to bend at the knees to see your face. If the mirror is too high, you have to stand on your toes to see if your belt buckle is on level.

Window size and placement have the same realities. To see a big view from deep in the interior of your home, the window needs to be relatively large. Similarly, to see beautiful hills in the distance, it's unwise to cut off the top side of that view by having the top of the window (known to construction nerds as its "head") set to the classic 6-ft. 8-in. door head height. When the view is big or distant or what you're looking at is tall, the larger opening makes sense. As well, if your view is down a hill, the lower the windowsill, the better. Note that this is an inside rule: The way your house opens from the outside may have to mud-wrestle with what you want to see from the inside.

Expand the Land

AN EARLY-19TH-CENTURY farmhouse was awkwardly added on to in the 1970s. Part of the awkwardness was a Ranch ell that dug itself into the rising hillside at the back of the house. By carefully excavating the gentle slope down to the level of the first floor to create a large terrace, the usable outside social area was doubled. New walls of windows and doors replaced isolated openings. The existing roofscape and fireplace were maintained, but a new one-story infill addition built between the 1970s addition and an early-20th-century extension created an opportunity for yet another glass wall opening out to the newly created exterior world, allowing the terrace to be completely meshed with the home's interior.

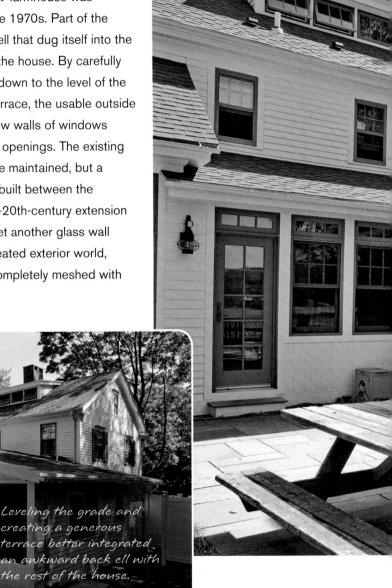

Leveling the grade and creating a generous terrace better integrated an awkward back ell with the rest of the house.

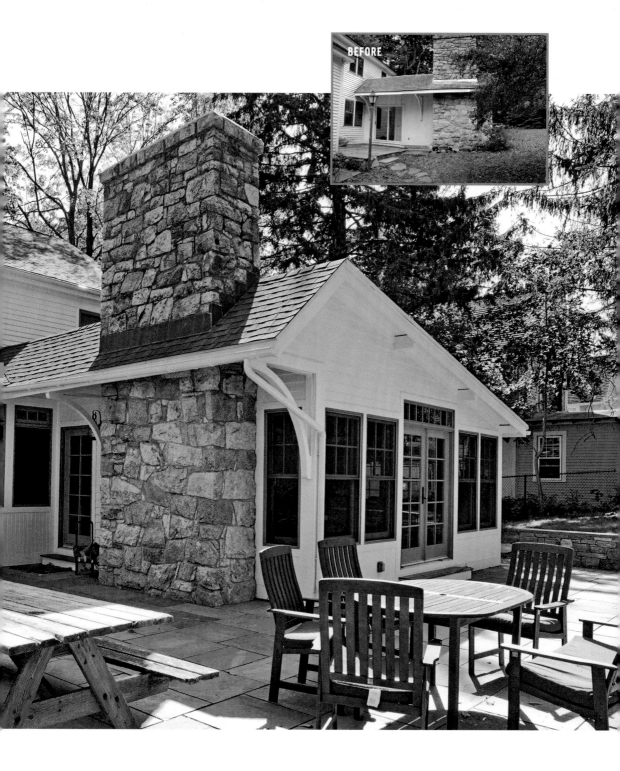

BEFORE

BEFORE

The view from inside.

dirt touching siding = rot

Dirt contains billions of little microbes that need to eat something organic to survive. Obviously, there are a lot of nutrients in dirt, but there are even better nutrients in the wood that your home is probably built of. With a little bit of dampness laid up against almost any wood that has not been fully pressure treated, rot will invade your house and have a good meal.

Dirt builds up around the foundation because people tend to overmulch, and over time dirt is piled up above the line where your siding stops. Even if your home is made of stucco or brick, it's a good idea to find out where the foundation ends and that hard surface begins. In the stucco, brick, or stone in most homes there's a veneer set over wood, and if dirt builds up against that material, water will find its way in and begin the process of decay.

Fortunately, the solution is simple and can be done by anyone with the strength of a 14-year-old: Simply shovel or rake away the built-up material until it's at least 6 in. (most experts say 12 in.) lower than wherever the wood part of your house begins—siding or structure.

Reaching Out from the 1920s

WHEN THIS BRICK center hall Colonial home was built in the 1920s, the designer didn't want its storage space for the then high-tech transportation system (automobiles) to present a gaping hole to the street; to conceal their presence, the cars were brought all the way around to the backyard in an extraordinarily awkward travel path. The new owners sought to change that pattern by reorienting the garage doors to face the street. This pragmatic, functional fix allowed the back wall of the garage to be a launching point for a new family room that was the counterpoint to the existing house—curving, vaulting, and all windows. One bold addition defeats the tight confines the 1920s brick skin imposed on all the existing windows, and by vaulting the ceiling the windows could rise to capture the full sweep of the backyard's plantings.

BEFORE

BEFORE   AFTER

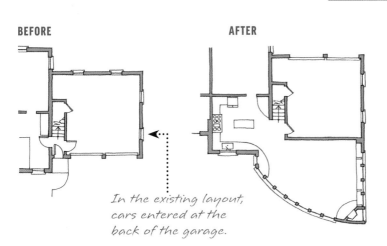

In the existing layout, cars entered at the back of the garage.

▶ go to **www.
staying
put.com**
to learn why
eaves save

All the new glass is protected by deep eaves, preventing glare, overheating, and rainwater coming into the house when windows are opened.

Celebrating a View

THE TWO MAIN GOALS for the remodel of this seaside home were to fix some chronic roof leaks and connect the house to the spectacular view. Recycling the foundation of a shallow-pitch, pop-on addition made in the 1970s helped get the more steeply pitched new roof through zoning. The steeper pitch of the roof helped prevent leaks, and its extended eaves keep super-heating summer sun at bay while protecting windows and doors from the ravages of seaside weather. New windows were sized to capture a very large view. In addition, a clunky diagonal upper deck was replaced by a simple balcony that is cantilevered and freestanding from the new roofscape.

BEFORE

Replacing the dropped beam and 2x8 floor framing of the existing upper deck with thick decking spanning between two new brackets opened up the view from the existing doors below.

BEFORE

If a house leaks, it is not a house anymore

It is a reasonable baseline assumption that when you pay the vast majority of your net worth to live in a house, it should keep you dry. Not leaking is a home's prime directive. Whether it is a flat roof's vain attempt to control gravity, a spec home's 27 different valleys all intersecting each other, or multiple generations of roof forms crashing into each other in an older home, when roofs are chronically leaky you don't live in a home anymore, you live in a sculpture that happens to have space in it where you seek refuge—but not comfort.

Getting Out of the House

YOU DON'T HAVE to add on to bring the outside in. When you keep the exterior walls in place, there is only one way to make a simple Cape reach out into the landscape: Create walls of windows. Given the fact that this particular Cape had one gable end facing the street with a garage and sun room addition tacked onto it, an internal fusion of the original home and its addition was necessary to fully appreciate the open side yard that was slowly becoming a garden of delights for the homeowners. One flowing space was made of an interior separated by a set of stairs, its two walls, and some interior partitions. Removing an awkward second-floor deck and its rude columns further opened up the visual connection.

BEFORE

Moving the front door to the opposite side of the house from the new window wall put the stairs, railings, and the doorway itself out of the visual flow.

You don't have to add on to **bring the outside in.**

Big View, Big Room

BEFORE

SOMETIMES YOU JUST have to add on to make the most of a site's potential. In this case, a center hall Colonial with a breezeway kitchen that attached to a garage turned its back on the wonderful view of a mountain to the south. A large informal living space was added with a gable end of windows so the homeowners could fully appreciate the previously ignored view. A large and simple deck was built around the perimeter of this new room to extend the addition's social capacity.

Further, the outside is brought into this home in a unique way, using an interior window well that brought light deep into the middle of the house. A monitor roof above the new room had its side walls filled with clerestory windows to bring daylighting all the way back to the existing home. This remodel is obviously a very large scale undertaking that had a considerable cost, but the truth is the site almost demanded this level of appreciation.

The existing house turned its back on the view; the remodeled house embraces it.

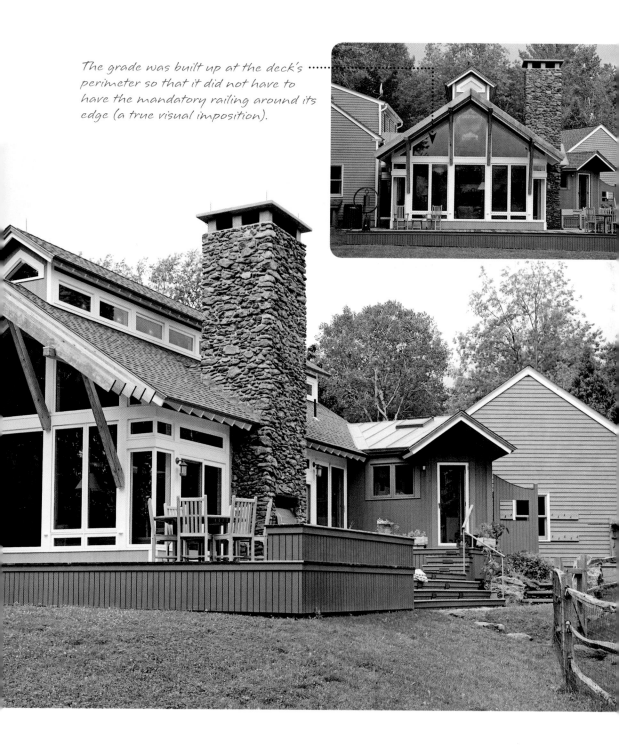

The grade was built up at the deck's perimeter so that it did not have to have the mandatory railing around its edge (a true visual imposition).

Discovering Your Inner Octagon

A CLASSIC FLAT-ROOFED family room was tacked onto a 1920s suburban home in the 1960s, its blank box walls punctured by stock windows that made this basic expansion claustrophobic. In a transformative gesture, an octagonal tower was inserted into the middle of the existing box with a lantern of clerestory windows popping up above the roof (now pitched and covered with standing seam metal to put an end to the never-ending leaks of the older roof). In addition, the exterior walls that were clad in grooved plywood gave way to windows and doors with mullions trimmed out in natural wood to simulate the half-timbering of this faux Tudor home.

BEFORE

The remodeled family room space.

In addition to the octagon tower, a large deck was built to reach between an existing terrace to one side and the back door on the other.

If it rains, flat roofs leak.

Go Up and Open Out

BEFORE

ZONING CODES CAN affect your remodel's exterior. This Cape had a classic awkward shed addition (built before zoning codes existed) as well as a three-season room/ screened porch wing and a filler deck. These early efforts to gain both space and view weren't wearing well and didn't maximize the beauty of the salt marsh backyard view. Expansion out was impossible as the home already was too wide and covered too much of the site, according to the Gods of Zoning.

The existing screened porch and three-season room were remade in place, and their roof provided an opportunity for a large second-floor balcony, all within the setback restriction and within the footprint. The porch was resurfaced, and a walk-out cantilevered deck was added above the existing deck. The biggest new connection to the outdoors was made by removing the existing shed-roofed second floor and raising the height of the first-floor ceiling to 9 ft. The new second floor had small bedrooms with high cathedral ceilings and wall-to-wall windows (kept under the height limit). The extra height made space for tall windows and glass doors to capture full views on both floors.

BEFORE

AFTER

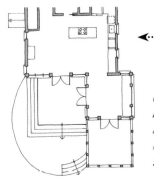

Everything built was created within the setback limits and over existing floor area— keeping to the current zoning limitations.

New second-floor outdoor
spaces included a long balcony
extended over the back wing
and a smaller cantilevered deck
off one of the bedrooms.

The existing den was converted into a higher-ceilinged three-season room, with double doors opening up to the revamped screened porch beyond.

BEFORE

Windows with hinges are better than windows that slide

Windows are the most vulnerable part of your home, especially the operable ones. They inherently cut into the watertight rain slicker that is your home's surface, and no amount of flashing or careful detailing can ultimately defeat the fact that you're cutting holes into a wall to get light and air in.

Windows that slide (double-hung windows or sliders) lose their ability to keep drafts out of your house more quickly than windows that are cranked shut and pulled tight (hinged units such as casements, awnings, or hoppers). Windows that open in are particularly problematic. Clad windows will always last longer than nonclad windows, but windows that are made purely out of vinyl have a "memory" and over time can change their shape, creating a less effective seal. Pulling tight against weatherstripping makes a better seal. Sliding against weatherstripping is inherently problematic and over time makes the seal less effective.

6

Bedrooms & bathrooms

For some people, a master suite is a place of repose to sleep and/or read; for others, it could mean a soaking tub that is not primarily about cleanliness. It could mean lighting that makes a mirror a thing that you don't fear. But mostly it means a place that doesn't frustrate you.

It's my professional experience that large-scale master suite remodeling projects have ceased to be a top priority for most homeowners.

There may be no direct reciprocal effect, but times of economic uncertainty are likely sobering enough that our need for pampering gets put on the back burner—at least that's what the anecdotal evidence suggests on how most homeowners are thinking about the places where they sleep and bathe.

When it comes to bedrooms, the focus now is on scale and detailing to create a very personal space as opposed to a bragging-rights showplace for the benefit of the rare visitor or the unknown potential buyer. This is the one room in the house where intimacy, craft, and accoutrement should help you get back in touch with yourself.

ABOVE: In this delightfully detailed master suite, sleeping space is separated from an office by a built-in storage unit, a dropped header, and a column.

The fundamental purpose of a master suite is to allow for sleep and that means a bed. In over 30 years as an architect, I have never designed a master suite around separate beds. I have had many couples who have a designated guest bedroom to allow a spouse to leave because of snoring (or maybe for reasons that are best left to the couples themselves to work out). Perhaps for similar

The fundamental purpose of a master suite is to allow for sleep and that means a bed.

In this above-garage master bedroom, an existing dormer was reinvented and surrounded by built-ins both to expand a visual space and to make a focal point for the bed that faced it. The painted built-ins and window seat were carefully woven between the low walls of the dramatic ceilingscape that resulted from expanding the dormer.

reasons, the size of the bed has grown over the years so that a queen is normal and a California king (7 ft. by 7 ft.!) is not unusual.

Like every other element of a home's interior, master bedrooms are increasingly linked to the outside world. Larger windows, a walk-out porch, or a first-floor location are becoming more common. The master suite ultimately should have the bed as the core. Sleeping takes the vast majority of time spent in our homes, not the kitchen, not the closet, not the sitting area. Increasingly, the master bedroom is a room for a bed, not a very large room with a bed in it that also accommodates a place to work out, sit, or learn dance steps. This house within a house has morphed into the most personal place within a home.

Bathrooms:
master and otherwise

Bathrooms and kitchens have a unique relationship. On the one hand, they both involve the complexities of plumbing, cabinetry, and surfaces, with the additional challenge of dealing with steamy air and unwanted odors in a bathroom make-over. On the other hand, they are polar opposites. The kitchen needs to be in constant visual contact with almost every public space in the house. However, privacy is a unique concern in bathroom design. While physical access is clearly important, bathrooms simply should not be visually accessible to any other space.

Since bathrooms are often set deep within a home's interior, showers, plumbing, and the need for mirrors over sinks makes it hard to accommodate windows. Skylights are a very effective way to provide natural light into a space that desperately needs it. In addition, overlighting and wall-to-ceiling mirrors help bounce light to project space beyond the physical barriers of the room.

That being said, no amount of light and reflection can overcome a bathroom whose toilet space is smaller than 3 ft. by 5 ft. Similarly, if there is not a full 2 ft. 6 in. or 3 ft. beyond the counter edge of the vanity or sink lip to the next element it encounters (whether it's a wall or even a toilet lip), things get a bit dicey, especially given the fact that many of us who need to wear contacts or glasses are without them when using a bathroom. As we grow older, the risk of tripping, falling, and slipping is greatly enhanced and therefore many renovations of bathrooms deal with universal design aspects that involve grab bars, integrated benches, and higher toilets and sinks.

A normal bathroom (5 ft. by 8 ft.) can temporarily make do as a master bath, but given the fact that most people would prefer to have a very large shower and a slightly oversize vanity, 5 ft. by 10 ft. or more has become the current master bathroom minimum. But no longer is there a need for a gigantic tub *and* a shower and a separate room for a toilet, let alone the Jack and Jill or his and her bath approach of infinite, ongoing redundancy.

Today's master bathrooms are designed to contour to the way couples use them. More couples than ever have different wake-up times, and therefore the bathroom often needs to have a second way out so that the early riser can leave without waking the slumbering spouse. The toilet in

ABOVE: Skylights are an effective way to provide natural light into a space that desperately needs it.

Sometimes you can turn a closet into a half-bath. In this cramped antique house, which had no room for expansion, a small closet presented itself as a location for a remote toilet as part of a larger master bath rehab. The closet was deep, elevated, and awkward, but with the expansion of its side wall the existing space was just big enough to allow for the installation of a toilet and sink. The existing door, steps, and HVAC all remain the same, and the use of wood paneling kept the effect more domestic than lavatory in sensibility.

a master suite is exquisitely personal because it is used by one or two people—*not* by everyone who comes into your house or by growing children. So a toilet with a view, a library, its own room, a telephone, or even a TV all become part of the personal choices of people who want to make their master suite a place away from the pull of career, family, and the rest of our culture's demands.

going geriatric

Just like our lifestyles, our homes are adapting as we age in place. Fewer of us can simply cash out and buy a snow bird paradise. If you are living in your home into your 70s, this could mean planning for an elevator, or it could mean thinking about where a new septic system needs to be located to accommodate a future ground-floor bedroom (perhaps the family room can become that bedroom).

Single-family homes have no code requirement for handicapped accessibility. In fact, the vast majority of people who have limited mobility do not use wheelchairs. Walkers, canes, or even just slower, more cautious movement is the rule for most people of a certain age, and given the nature of the boomer generation the overall level of fitness will mean that designing in a 7/11 (7-in. rise and 11-in. tread) stair with railings on both sides will probably answer the needs of most people planning to spend the foreseeable future in a multistory home. But planning where an access ramp could go or allowing for wide doors and easy passage between rooms makes good sense.

One other thing that might encourage you to retrofit an elevator or a ramp is the resale value. While there are more of them now, there are still few houses that have master bedrooms down. Accessible kitchens or baths that allow people with limited mobility to see that they have a future in a home for many years are remarkable features. The more you prepare for those late times and your long-term occupancy, the more you open up the market for your house.

Family bathrooms

The other bathrooms present in a home need to accommodate the most fundamental of human needs but also a variety of schedules. This often means that bathrooms that were once completely open and always contained a tub but only one sink now have separate toilet and shower areas, two sinks, and perhaps even a little closet within its walls to enfold all the different commodities that get used (not just linens but toiletries as well). This means 5 ft. by 10 ft. is often the minimum size for the family bathroom, too.

Given that this bathroom will likely be used by teenagers, surfaces should be more durable than in a master bathroom. You typically need to provide solid surfaces that can't be chipped or worn through (lacquered cabinets are a real no-no). Solid-surface countertops, impact-resistant, laminated cabinet fronts, and heavy-duty tiles (with nonwhite grout) work best. Shelves above vanities are just as important as medicine cabinets (especially for visitors) to capture the vast quantity of overflow that can happen when more than two people use the bathroom.

Like kitchens, bathroom remodels have the ability to completely overwhelm a budget. The surfaces are inherently expensive, and the need to custom-fit all those surfaces within a tight envelope and interweave mechanical systems means there's a large window of vulnerability for error. Just like a kitchen, when a bathroom works, it is sublime. But when a bathroom design is a mess, it is a never-ending source of frustration, anger, and, unlike the kitchen, personal embarrassment.

BELOW: Squeezing this new bath into an existing bedroom space in a remodeled traditional home was made possible by leaving existing windows in place, doubling up vanities as furniture, and installing a full-glass transparent shower.

One Move Changes Everything

IN A CLASSIC 1960s home, two bedrooms were combined to make one master suite with a full walk-in closet. With a watchful eye on cost, just one big move transformed predictable sleeping quarters into a restful retreat. A boldly sized, expressively designed window replaced two typical small-scale units. Given that this is a one-story wing extended off the existing two-story home, the ceiling could be lightly vaulted to angle to the existing roof above. The vaulted ceiling area accommodates three custom-angled transom windows, which are tight to the new ceiling, allowing natural light to bounce into the sleeping space. The resulting open space not only embraces the new window but also comfortably supports the owners' king-size bed.

BEFORE

AFTER

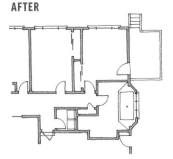

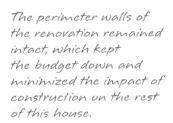

Taking out the closet walls between two existing bedrooms created an open master bedroom with plenty of space to accommodate a new walk-in closet.

The perimeter walls of the renovation remained intact, which kept the budget down and minimized the impact of construction on the rest of this house.

Trim lines extend around the room based on the division between the new window array's operable units below and the fixed transoms above.

One big move transformed predictable sleeping quarters into a restful retreat.

The Beauty of Built-Ins

BEFORE

WHEN FLOOR AREA is limited, you need to "dense up" your storage, and in this regard built-ins are better at packing clothing into a small space than are closets. In an extremely tight existing Bungalow-style home where the roof imposed itself on virtually every upstairs space, a very small bedroom could gain the required storage capacity only by carefully placing built-ins on the outside wall (and precisely allocating the space available under the roofline for closets). An existing shed dormer provided not only a place for windows on two walls but also more space to install built-ins under the roof beyond its outside wall. It took a great deal of on-paper master planning, but in the end built-in cabinetry allowed for bookcases, HVAC ducting, hanging closet space, and a window seat.

The surgical insertion of built-ins minimized the need for free-standing furniture.

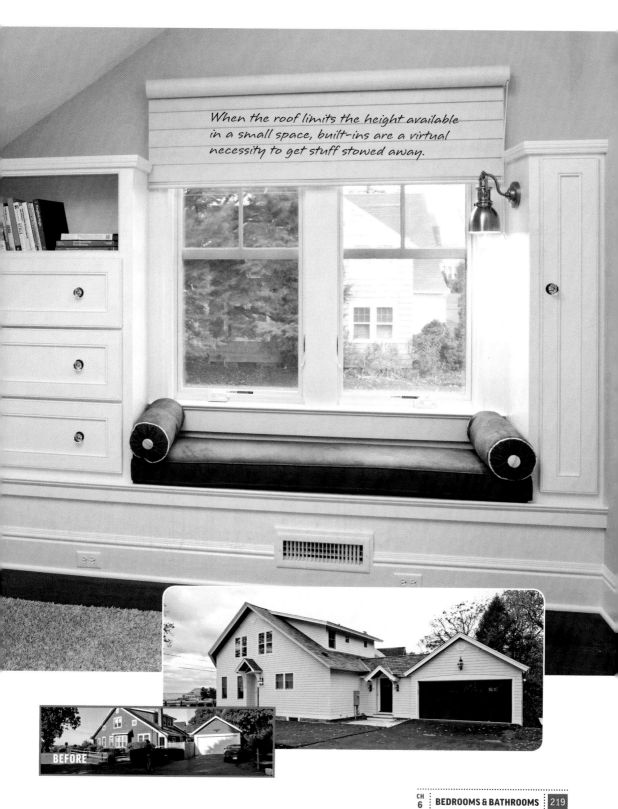

When the roof limits the height available in a small space, built-ins are a virtual necessity to get stuff stowed away.

BEFORE

PROJECT Creating a Place Inside

WHEN AN EMPTY-NESTER couple downsized to a 1980s condo, they realized that they needed to create a place for themselves when visiting children (and potentially their children's children) invaded their new space. So the owners commandeered the entire middle floor of their condo, leaving the lower floor for the returning offspring and the uppermost floor for the home office (shown on pp. 262–263). As with most condos, the middle of the plan was fairly dim, and therefore they opted to use a large sliding-glass door at the top-lit stairs to allow some natural light into the middle of their floor. The front side of the condo (which originally had a bedroom and a small bath) was given over entirely to a bath and expanded laundry space.

The back view side is occupied by the master bedroom suite in two portions—a sleeping space with a large bed and fixed stone side tables and, at the other side, a new closet set to the inside of the plan with a vaulted meditation space to the outside. Given that no windows could be changed or moved, the owners found self-expression through trim and detail.

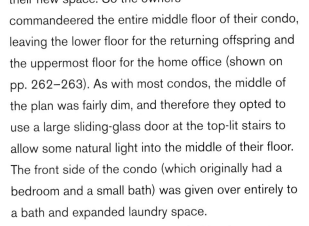

BEFORE

These days, bedrooms are increasingly just rooms for beds.

The barebones sleeping space features fixed stone side tables and wall-mounted reading lights.

Opposite the glass sliding door, a custom set of cabinet closets helps accommodate the storage needed when downsizing happens.

A large sliding-glass door at the top-lit stair allows natural light to filter into the middle of the couple's floor.

BEFORE

Bedroom

AFTER

Extraordinary custom detailing and mirror work make the tight bathroom at the front of the condo visually sustainable.

Bringing the Outside In

CONTEMPORARY HOMES don't often lend themselves well to additions. In this 1970s Contemporary, a notch cut into the wedge roof created a second floor walk-out porch. In keeping with the modern zeitgeist, that porch had a flat roof, and following the laws of physics the roof always leaked. The new owners of the house wanted to maintain the exquisite view to the salt marsh, but they also wanted to create a place for meditation and a loft where their visiting grandchildren could have fun. By filling in the cut-out corner with a fully glazed double-height sun room, the view was saved, leaks were prevented, and a small loft was provided for the grandkids. This new infill piece has its roof popped above the wedge and given a rakishly enhanced angle and an even more zesty eaves extension—4 ft. to one side and 2 ft. to the other, following the angular modern aesthetic but also helping protect the big windows from the coastal climate.

BEFORE

The new sunspace and loft off the existing studio preserve the wonderful view over the marsh.

BEFORE

Let sleeping shapes lie

When renovating a house, it's very easy to get excited about making big changes: raising the roof, making a facade symmetrical, or angling out a wall. But with an existing shell that's comfortable in its own skin and has systems that are closed circuits (plumbing, electricity, HVAC), it's much more cost-effective to think about alternatives to expanding your house. If you just have to make your house bigger, brainstorm simple discreet ways to do it. For example, it's better to tee off an existing form rather than reinvent its shape; and rather than cutting halfway into a Cape and making an addition through the existing roof, it's much easier to tack something onto its gable end.

POTENTIALLY DARK, and potentially depressing, basement baths need special attention. Lighting is one of the key issues, and artificial lighting has to be enhanced because there is little opportunity for natural daylighting. Storage can also be problematic in a tight basement bath. Here, cabinetry is not only under the sink, and on either side of it, but there is also a deep medicine cabinet set over the sink and a linen closet at the head of the tub. As in any basement renovation, waste lines that depend on gravity need to be accommodated in the concrete floor. But even allowing for selective removal and replacement of the floor, this remodel project was considerably cheaper than if a new bathroom had been added to the footprint of the home.

Just because it's a basement bath, don't think that style doesn't matter. The curving lines of the stone countertop and the dropped soffit above are anything but industrial in sensibility.

BEFORE

In a potentially dim basement space, it's important to capture whatever natural light is available (the thin window at top right) and supplement with plenty of artificial lighting.

Building inside the Box

IN A CLASSIC urban loft, bedroom and bathroom space was created out of the open plan of a former factory building. With only one wall of significant natural light, it made sense to use large upper-level transoms to bring the light into the new spaces. Given that maintaining privacy was important, a double-walled

BEFORE

exterior glazing material was used for those transoms; as a bonus, the glass also provides a good level of sound suppression. By making the new partitions for the bedroom out of inexpensive, clear-finished, maple-veneered plywood, the new construction plays off of the existing factory's columns and white walls and ceilings. As is typical with many factories, refinished birch floors serve as a lively organic base for the simple linear millwork that created the bedroom wall.

BEFORE

AFTER

Living, bedroom, and bathroom space was created out of the open plan of a former factory building.

In the new bathroom, both mirror and simple linear tilework maximize the sense of space while providing tough materials to resist teenagers' onslaughts.

The partition between the living room (foreground) and bedroom was built to create a space that was private but allowed ambient light to fill its interior. With operable transoms, the natural flow of air makes the bedroom feel less cloistered.

In the new bedroom, a wall of built-ins accommodates space for study and storage.

The shared computer station layered on the outside wall of the bedroom is a literal side benefit.

7

Front entries & mudrooms

The classic setup: An unused front door (at left) is usurped by a welcoming side entry adjoining the garage and driveway.

There is an odd reality in America, perhaps one of the strangest unspoken misfits in all of architecture.

It's been over 100 years since people used horses to get around, yet more than half of the homes in America have a front door facing the street even though 90 percent of those who enter the house come in from the driveway.

Millions upon millions of homes have front walkways that start out pointing toward the street for about 10 ft. or 15 ft. and then take a hard turn to go to where all of the action actually happens: the driveway. When you think about it, this is an absurd and silly vestigial nod to a time that is so far gone that we have no idea that it ever was.

Open flagstone steps replace high-maintenance wood steps on this remodeled entry, allowing better access and more freedom of movement.

Making a centered, symmetrical facade is the norm; making something that faces sideways or skews to the actual point of entry (that is, the cars) is seen as contemporary. But there are ways you can deal with the anomaly of having an entry face the street that no one ever uses. These involve landscape gestures where a large-scale turn can happen, lighting, and careful level changes if your home is on a hilly site.

The front entry is our prom dress—designed to dazzle or at least to impress.

before &
AFTER

Shedding water and providing shelter are important parts of greeting visitors, and front entries should allow for these polite gestures.

Combining entries

There are radical solutions, however, that allow the back door and front door to fuse, by either relocating the mudroom to a position near the front door or by simply making a side/back door so prominent and well designed that it can have the presence and power of a typical front door. This can take some radical rethinking, but that's exactly what you need in homes that are terminally misconstrued and misfitting in the way they are used.

ABOVE & RIGHT: Mudrooms are no longer blank spaces where furnishings are screwed to the wall but actually have integrated millwork and highly durable permanent installations of storage facilities.

Redirecting flow can have unfortunate consequences because muddy shoes, sweaty work-out clothes, and compost-drenched gardening gear must be headed off at the mudroom instead of bringing the mess into a place where you'd rather be clean and smell-free. Therefore, laundries often gravitate to the side locations (clearly hampers should), and if you have children, large-scale lockers can give knapsacks, book bags, and class projects a home so they aren't left in the kitchen.

where are they now? good-bye to the space that said hello

Double-height and triple-hyped gigantic entry hall boxes with a staircase on steroids that uses almost every part from the catalog have come to mock their owners in silent uselessness. The giant chandelier made from every leftover piece of brass piping from a Chinese conduit factory and festooned with bazillions of glass bead cascades has crashed of its own weight. Mansion-envy entries in entry-level homes were absurd on their face and are not viable.

In the land where most of us live, suburbia, we don't use our front doors because they often are far from our driveways. The front entry is our prom dress—designed to dazzle or at least to impress, but ultimately uncomfortable and a source of regret after it was impulsively purchased.

What can the homeowner do with this huge airbag of unused and now guilt-ridden ostentatious showiness? These spaces can become galleries for the art that you've kept in the attic, but you need to provide lighting specific to each painting. Their blank walls can benefit greatly from trim or paneling or surface treatments that break up their boxiness (as shown on pp. 252–253). Floating windows on the upper level need to be tethered to the ceiling and front door with trim that's tied into the rest of the space.

These thoughtless stage-sets designed as sales tools rather than as functional entries are hard to deal with, but they can be visually neutered with some careful detailing to make them yours.

Entry and mudroom surfaces clearly need to wear well, with wainscoted walls, tile-tough floors, and durable surfaces to sit on. And these side entries now have an imperative of beauty that they never had before because front doors are today used only for holidays and major family events (think Thanksgiving and weddings).

So the twin realities of formal front and useful side entries are being merged, and the toxic qualities of either (the antiquated street-facing front with the often disheveled, chaotic, and beat-up mudroom) can have their most egregious anomalies smoothed over.

PROJECT Entering at a Split

THE CHALLENGE: How to make a sheltering, welcoming entry at the awkward fracture between the two parts of a Split Ranch. As is the case with this classic 1960s suburban home, nothing about the two sides of a Split Ranch aligns—neither windows, roofs, nor floors. These architectural discomforts can be exacerbated if the house is not built on a flat site. This Split Ranch is built on a hill so it was important to create a welcoming entry. To this end, a new cantilevered gabled roof was built to project beyond the existing front door. The change is remarkable for what remained unchanged—the door itself, and all the elements around the door (roofs, walls, and windows).

BEFORE

AFTER

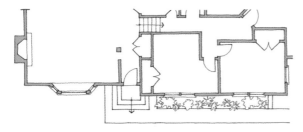

The entry walk was widened to 6 ft. to make a gracious turn into the house from the driveway rather than a hard right-angle marching-band pivot.

When a house is built on an elevated site, the entry grabs a lot of attention when seen from below.

find your home: the ranch

The first Ranch was a single-story affair built by a man named Cliff May in San Diego in 1932. The idea was to build a home that was as affordable as possible to fit the minimal needs of Depression-era families. What made this building a Ranch? Hard to say, but it has a layout that's evenly split between bedrooms on one side and living space on the other, with low-pitched roofs and broad eaves.

The incredibly bland, bourgeois-friendly Ranch proliferated across the United States in the 1950s, and the gist of its exterior aesthetics and interior organization can be traced directly to Frank Lloyd Wright's Prairie houses. It was as if fine Szechwan cooking were interpreted by La Choy®. The greatest outrage for Frank was when the one-story Ranch became the Raised Ranch, with story-and-a-half or two-story walls, completely violating every aesthetic tenant of the Prairie-style horizontality.

Ranch homes today represent almost the worst of all worlds: a home that is bisected like a center hall Colonial and constrictive like a Cape. Because Ranches are often split-level homes, or one-floor homes with bedrooms on one side and living space on the other, there's virtually no opportunity to escape the straitjacket of their extreme plan limitations.

The new entry roof uses a 4-ft. projection to cast shadows to draw attention, but at night lighting below marvelously illuminates its ceilingscape. A new diamond window further enhances the effect.

The new wood steps replaced the old precast stock concrete stoop and have their treads wrapped around an entry platform, which frees them from the need for railings.

Getting Attention from a Distance

TO DRAW ATTENTION to a front door that is high above a street filled with heavy traffic, sometimes you need to go big and bold. A classic symmetrically centered home facing a very busy suburban street was set about 25 ft. above street level. In addition, the delicately diminutive existing front entry was rotting, and there was precious little closet space or room to take coats off once anyone walked into the front door.

A dramatic gesture was called for in the form of a larger, more expressive entry. The interior impact was limited to the centered window directly above the old front door, which had to have its sill raised (fortunately, it was in a bathroom). This one accommodation allowed the interior space at the front door location to pop out 4 ft. from the existing brick facade. A new front door was surrounded by glass, with a full set of upper transoms and flanking side lights. The scale and broad openness of the new entry and the curves of the transom and the support brackets also drew attention to an entry that in the past was easily missed.

BEFORE

Bumping out the front entry made room for matching closets at either side and flooded the space with light.

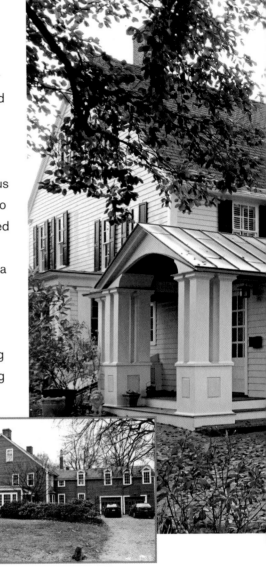

IN A CENTER HALL Colonial set on a New England town green, the symmetrically located front door was never used. An ell-wing garage addition was built onto the main house in the 1920s, but while there was plenty of room for cars there was precious little accommodation for those entering the house to get cover from the elements. A side door was tacked on in the 1970s, an unheated 3-ft. by 3-ft. airlock, with a door going directly (and inconveniently) into a bay built for informal dining.

The new side entry extension has four-square columns to support its porch roof. The four-square aesthetic was applied to the existing informal dining bay and the exterior trim of the garage, transforming the entire side of the house from apologetically ad hoc to coordinately remodeled. The new 6-ft. by 10-ft. entry expansion allowed for a mudroom with built-ins and a new closet. Windows both inside and out and a 12-paned glass door were used to make the transition from outside to inside a light-filled experience.

BEFORE

When you think about remodeling your home, it doesn't necessarily have to be picture perfect.

The new entry replaces a side door that originally entered through the dining room bay.

The new 6-ft. by 10-ft. entry expansion allowed for a mudroom with built-ins and a new closet.

Style is not a religion: flexible aesthetics help

Stick-built American homes are genius in their flexibility. However, when an extremely rigid style (academically perfect Classical, historically perfect Colonial, consistently frenetic Victorian, pristinely abstracted Modernism) ends up making mountains out of mole hills of perfected details, orientations, scales, and alignments, things can get very expensive. If the perfect is necessary, it will be the enemy of the good, and often striving for perfection in renovating a house means that the renovation ends up being so costly when bid that nothing happens. So when you think about remodeling your home, know that although its style may be charming, it doesn't necessarily have to be picture perfect. If your home is its own Bible, Quran, or Torah, it may be time for a little heresy.

Sometimes Detail Is All You Need

BLANK GARAGE DOORS do not have to be your guests' first impression of your home. On the original house, a classic Raised Split Ranch, the equally classic half-level entry was covered by an extension of one side of the gable roof over the garage half of the split. Sadly, the front door lost the visual competition for those visiting the home to bland, street-level double garage doors with a sad out-of-the-catalog bay window set above them. Fortunately, the wall above the garage was cantilevered a few feet beyond the door wall, putting the garage doors in shade.

With a limited budget three things were done: First, a trellis was added over the garage doors to cast them even further in shade and provide a nicely detailed decorative touch. Second, a new gable roof was applied over the stock bay window that mimics the major gable roof above that side of the house. And last, the existing roof that simply hung over the entry was visually returned to create a low-cost decorative "gable trellis" made with clear stained pressure-treated wood, to match the new garage door detail. Otherwise the door, steps, walk, and other elements of the entry remained unchanged.

BEFORE

Blank garage doors do not have to be your guests' first impression of your home.

Adding trellises over the entry and garage doors and a new gable roof over the upper-level bay window transforms the entry to this Split Ranch without blowing the budget.

Moving the Entry Can Make Sense

BEFORE

STOCK PLANS ARE designed with the idea that the front door faces the street and the site is flat. So entries for these homes can be problematic if either of these conditions is not met. A Cape that had its gable end facing the street had an apologetic side entry laid up against and into a sun room under a garage that was set on the downhill side. An entirely new approach was called for to overcome these twin misfits of grade and plan orientation.

The existing entry was removed and a new one built on the other side of the house so that it could more directly serve the existing kitchen and provide a gentle elevating set of steps to get up to the first floor. What was sacrificed was a bizarrely oversize bathroom/laundry room. The new entryhall was taken out of that double-duty space, with the bathroom losing a tub but keeping the toilet location to become a three-quarter bath.

On the outside, decorative brackets, a decorative light fixture, and natural wood give this simple entry a sense of detail and focus that rewards those who drive onto the tight site.

BEFORE

AFTER

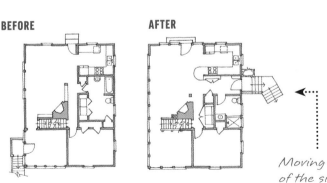

Existing entry.

Moving the entry to the uphill side of the site required some regrading, as well as modifications to the existing bathroom/laundry.

The new entry roof is set high to be visible from the street 60 ft. away; the added height allows for a clerestory window that gets light into the new entryhall.

IN A LARGE-SCALE center hall Colonial built in the 1980s, the double-height space is often a stark undecorated airbag. You could hang art, you could apply a jazzy wallpaper, or you could let a gigantic chandelier draw attention away from the overscale room. But those moves do not change the space's awkward scale, and they may even accentuate it. This particular entry was brought together by the use of trim designed in connecting lines to form paneling. Rather than a stylistic appliqué of wood or wallpaper, this trim takes its cues from the existing lines of the second floor and the existing first-floor openings and was carefully integrated to create locations for lighting, mirrors, and furniture.

Using trim designed to resemble paneling is a lot less expensive than applying full wood panels.

BEFORE

BEFORE

What was once a blank box of drywall, stock trim, and inadequate attention to detail is transformed to create an elegant ambiance.

8

Working at home

This fully operational home office was created in an existing attic.

Before the Industrial Revolution, the vast majority of people worked where they lived.

Where there was a farm or a small business, the idea of commuting was unknown as we were all "localvores." Obviously, the Industrial Revolution and, ultimately, the automobile, threw that idea out the window.

But the next revolution is upon us. Today, most people use the Internet and computers at work . . . and at home. In short, we are in the middle of a revolution that has had and will continue to have just as much impact as the steam engine, harnessing electricity, and inventing steel had over 100 years ago. And typically when a technical or physical change is that universal, the impact resonates down into where we live.

This online, all-the-time availability of work when brought home can ruin both. So the home office that could just as easily be a laptop (on your lap) has created a new place in the American home. Intentionally out of sight and mind when not in use, some home offices need direct access to the outside, others need to be hermetically sealed from the sounds and chaos of family life, and all of them need the ability to safely harbor the technology that allows the luxury of staying put.

Home offices that are viewed with disdain and ushered into a basement or a closet tend to make labor not only exhausting but also simply nasty.

What makes our generation's version of the home office distinctive is that it can actually be quite small, even just a piece of furniture. Since paper is becoming passé, the home office can literally be a built-in. It can be shuttered up and visually kept out of our line of sight when we are off-duty.

However, home offices that are viewed with disdain and ushered into a basement or a closet tend to make labor not only exhausting but also simply nasty. The ability to look up from the computer screen every once in a while, catch a breath of fresh air, or simply put your feet up

has made design an imperative for many home offices. Horizontal surfaces that are flexible with open knee space underneath them allow for numerous arrangements so that chaos can be controlled or even embraced without embarrassment.

In the past, the vast majority of typical Americans kept all work at arm's length. Many homes had studies, but these typically had at least one and sometimes two doors through which any number of people could walk at any given time of day to get from the kitchen to the living room. What's clear is that limited access and segregation from noise are now essential even in the most domesticated office, so portions of attics can be good points of opportunity or even a modest addition can support home office activity at a minimum cost . . . and may be tax-deductible at that (if you've got a good accountant).

ABOVE: Tucked into a corner of a small addition, a new custom-built desk created a stealth office in an open interior. When its doors are closed, the visual effect is that this corner cabinet is a piece of furniture. When the unit's upper doors are opened and a pullout key pad drawer is extended, an office is revealed, as are vast quantities of paper products and supplies. (Private storage doesn't need to be kept perfectly ordered when you have the ability to shut the cabinet front to obscure the chaos of day-to-day life from visitors.)

Making the Home Office Work

A WING WAS ADDED onto a suburban home in the 1980s with the expressed intent of creating a home office. It filled that function relatively well until the new owner, who would also be using it as a home office, realized that the intensity of her work was so extreme that the existing built-ins were simply inadequate and the resulting visual chaos of stacks and stacks of papers and books set upon every horizontal surface (including the floor) could not be tolerated. The solution was a simple one: laminating an entire wall with deep cabinet storage and another wall with bookcases. All windows and doors stayed the same and only one closet was removed.

BEFORE

BEFORE

A library ladder runs on a rail to give access to the full available storage space on three walls (which climb to 12 ft. at the gable peak).

A new built-in desk was installed
at the old desk's original location.

IN MANY TRADITIONAL HOMES, dormers are essentially small portholes of light and ventilation in attic spaces; they were never intended to be used as functioning spaces but merely to help get light and air into an otherwise hot and dark space. In this 1920s suburban brick home, a classic doghouse dormer sat above a garage. The space above the garage was used as an office, and the lack of light (and the lack of space itself in an area that was dominated by angled ceilings) was solved by simply expanding the existing dormer to become a full desk space. Costs were saved by keeping one side of the existing dormer opening in the slate roof intact and by expanding the dormer opening in only one direction.

BEFORE

The new triple window array fills the full width of the larger dormer.

The expanded dormer is slightly off-center (which was good for the budget), but only a keen eye would notice.

BEFORE

Getting a Bonus

THE TOP FLOOR of a 1980s condominium unit was listed as a "bonus" space. It was unfinished, and at the top of the stair the door was set precariously close to the top tread. New owners decided to finish the space off as a home office, incorporating its additional potential as a guest room and meditation space. Given its location, the owners realized that in remodeling the loft, they could actually improve the ambiance of the floor below as well.

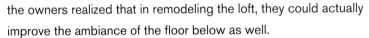

The tight door was removed, and a new wall at the top of the stairs allowed for a 3-ft. platform in front of a new door. In addition, the dormer that looked out to an extraordinary view had its floor raised two steps so that the person sitting at the desk could see out the windows. Next, bookcases were built in at various locations, as was a very tight three-quarter bath. Finally, the nondormer side of the space had its side walls opened up to take the light from a shed dormer at the top of the stairwell down to the master bedroom suite below.

BEFORE

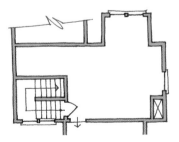

AFTER

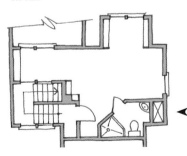

The new space comprised not only the home office but also a guest room, meditation space, and small bath.

The top floor of the condo was originally unfinished.

The working view.

To learn more about the demise of the bonus room ▶ go to www.stayingput.com

Afterword

Shakedown Cruise

So you planned, budgeted, contracted, and lived through the stress and chaos of remodeling. Now what?

You must first realize that no construction project is built perfectly—it simply can't be. There are too many complications, and you have to rely on too many suppliers of materials and services to be 100 percent certain that every aspect of the home will work perfectly forever. But fortunately, just like a new car, the work on your house has a series of warranties if things go awry.

Most states have a series of consumer protection laws that not only protect you from a builder's abuse during construction but also keep the builder legally obligated to fix his or her mistakes for a certain period (typically one year) from the time the job is finished. There are several definitions of the word finished. First, there is the date when you move back in (you should record this date in writing). Second, there is something that architects call substantial completion, which is when all the work that's on the drawings and in the contract is essentially complete. Third, there is the date of your final payment to the builder. Finally, there is the issuance by the town of a certificate of occupancy, which officially allows you to live in the house (and officially allows the town to greatly increase your taxes). Find out which date applies to your state's warranty provision or is cited in your contract with the builder.

Be aware that no warranty covers your son throwing a bowling ball through the wall. But if a door sticks, a joint in your trim opens up, or a hump develops in your floor, the builder is usually legally on the hook to deal with it. If you used a general contractor, he or she is responsible for the warranties of all the people that he or she hired to work on your house. If your paint peels after the job is done, you do not call the painter, you call the general contractor who will in turn call the painter. That is the GC's obligation and part of his or her warranty to you.

All the products and appliances that are in your home have some sort of manufacturer's warranty that is in effect only if the product is installed exactly the way the manufacturer specifies. If the product was installed properly and it doesn't work, you have recourse; you'll never get all the repairs done for free, but at least you'll get a product replacement and maybe some allowance for its installation. Be sure you have all those warranties in your hand before the builder leaves the site. But remember there are limitations to these warranties, too. If that same bowling ball hits your stove, the stove manufacturer is not obligated to replace it. But if you turn on a burner and it doesn't work and it falls within the warranty period of the appliance (typically a year or two), you can probably get it fixed at a lower cost than if it happens after the warranty runs out.

Beyond fixing things that do not function, your mind-set should be that you are test-driving a new appliance to see what works and what doesn't, what lives up to your expectations and what doesn't. Just as you took charge when you decided to undertake the remodeling, you need to take charge to make sure that the final product has a permanent reality that will stand you in good stead for all the years in your house that you see in front of you.